CONTENTS

Poems

Gallery

Essay

Poems

Reviews

The Poetry Review

The Poetry Society, 22 Betterton Street, London WC2H 9BX

The Poetry Review

The Poetry Society, 22 Betterton Street, London WC2H 9BX
Tel: +44 (0)20 7420 9880 • Fax: +44 (0)20 7240 4818
Email: poetryreview@poetrysociety.org.uk
poetrysociety.org.uk/thepoetryreview

Guest Editor: Colette Bryce
Production: Michael Sims

ISBN: 978-1-911046-19-6 ISSN: 0032 2156
Cover artwork: Marion Kadi, marionkadi.com
Cover quote by Alice Miller, see p. 15

The Poetry Review, The Poetry Society & contributors, 2019

. . .

SUBMISSIONS
We welcome submissions. Please follow
the guidelines which can be found at
poetrysociety.org.uk/thepoetryreview

ADVERTISING
To place advertisements, visit
poetrysociety.org.uk/thepoetryreview or
contact Oliver Fox on +44 (0)20 7420 9886,
email: marketing@poetrysociety.org.uk

BOOKSHOP DISTRIBUTION
Central Books, 50 Freshwater Road, London
RM8 1RX, UK. Tel: +44 (0)20 8525 8800
or visit centralbooks.com

PBS OFFER TO POETRY SOCIETY MEMBERS
The Poetry Book Society offers Poetry Society
Members a special 10% discount (plus postage)
on books bought from poetrybooks.co.uk.
For details and to obtain the discount code,
please contact Paul McGrane on
+44 (0)20 7420 9881.

SUBSCRIPTIONS & SALES
UK individuals: £38 / Europe: £48
Rest of the World: £53 (overseas delivery by airmail)
Single issue: £9.50 plus postage. Order from
poetrysociety.org.uk/shop or contact Paul McGrane
on +44 (0)20 7420 9881. Pay by cheque
(sterling and US dollar cheques only),
credit card or Direct Debit.

Subscribe to the digital version of *The Poetry
Review* at exacteditions.com/thepoetryreview
The Poetry Review is on sale in leading bookshops.
It is also available on audio CD.

The Poetry Review is the magazine of
The Poetry Society and was first published in 1912.
A subscription to *The Poetry Review* is included as
part of membership of The Poetry Society. Views
expressed in *The Poetry Review* are not necessarily
those of The Poetry Society; those of individual
contributors are not necessarily those of the Editor.

Charity Commission No. 303334.

. . .

THE**POETRYSOCIETY**

Supported using public funding by
**ARTS COUNCIL
ENGLAND**

EDITORIAL

While guest editing this issue I've been aware that we are in the final days of, to borrow Auden's phrase, "a low dishonest decade". In the small time-warp between sign off and the freshly delivered boxes of *The Poetry Review* being sliced open and copies despatched to our subscribers, another general election will have passed and things will be worse. Or better. Or something. The impeachment process in the US will have progressed, and things will be better. Or worse, etc. From this juncture in late November 2019, the outlook isn't inspiring. "Some days I wake up angry at everything", opens one poem in these pages. "When I hear what is happening in America" begins another, a poem about parental fear and personal responsibility.

With a certain synchronicity, Margaret Atwood has been touring with a new instalment of her famous dystopia. In conversation at the Sage Gateshead she is on characteristic good form. The audience, too many to conduct a conventional Q&A, is invited to tweet questions for the author, some of which concern the rise in authoritarianism that partly inspired her return to the story. The final question "Can you sort out Brexit for us?" is perhaps not entirely the joke it seems to be, for who better than a master of plot to envisage a way out, a good ending? Atwood laughs and then says something both wise and useful. "We're in a least worst scenario right now. Ask yourself what is the worst, then what's the next step up from the worst, and so on. Vote for the least worst."

"The best lack all conviction" wrote Yeats one hundred years ago, "while the worst / Are full of passionate intensity". Another audience has gathered at the Ilkley Literature Festival where a panel of poets is discussing 'The Second Coming' from which these much-quoted lines are taken. Written in the aftermath of the First World War and at the outset of the Irish War of Independence, the poem, like Auden's 'September 1, 1939' (see p. 51), is one that people have turned to at times of political crisis. It has been quoted more often since 2016 and the election of Donald Trump than ever in its hundred-year existence. Yeats later gave himself credit for predicting – in its lines – the rise of fascism in Europe, although it's something of a stretch to believe that this could have been foreseeable in 1919.

The poem's resonance a century on is uncanny. 'The Second Coming' summons in twenty-two lines our deepest human fears, of ourselves and the harm of which we're capable. Once again, the fog of Brexit hangs above the auditorium. There is a sense of a country trapped in suspended animation by the false binary imposed upon it: *which side are you on?* a national obsession as "things fall apart". One panellist, the poet Martina Evans, lightens the mood with Yeats's description in 'Nineteen Hundred and Nineteen' of a certain "insolent fiend": "There lurches past, his great eyes without thought / Under the shadow of stupid straw-pale locks". Yeats might gain some points for prophecy after all.

This winter, poems have arrived from all corners of the UK, Europe, the US and elsewhere. Some have, woven into their lines, the anxieties of our extraordinary moment – the climate emergency another pressing fear that has found expression in 2019 – while others dream, sing, make mischief – do all of the things that poems get up to. Poets yet to publish a full collection make up a third of those featured here. In our prose pages, Maria Johnston listens closely to the music of Denise Riley and Jeremy Noel-Tod weighs up the Auden of 'September 1, 1939' against other – sometimes conflicting – Audens. Lastly, we carry reviews of the great variousness of poetry collections finding their way to readers this winter. It has been a joy to stand in for Emily Berry and to work with the team at Betterton Street to produce this one-off issue. My thanks particularly to the indefatigable Mike Sims whose knowledge of this publication knows no bounds. I hereby hand over my findings and wish you a peaceful new year and a good read.

Colette Bryce

NICK LAIRD

The Mixed Marriage

Poetry's the art of introducing words
that haven't met before and getting them
to sit down in a room and agree terms
or fall in love or try to kill each other,
or first one thing and then the other.

Intermittently we knew it, the thready
lining at the bottom of the pocket of
astonishment, amongst small change
and balls of fluff. The best of the rest
of the time we kept our heads down

and tried to make sense, standing slightly
to the left of. But look how the words
are getting along – like a house on fire,
like a street of houses, like a cityscape
erupting now with sirens and flames.

On Form

Standing at pump four
of the garage in Ballydehob
filling the Honda with diesel,
I want the counter to stop
at a round number, a whole euro,
so if the tank's getting full
and the flow's clicking off
I restart, easing out my finger
then tightening the trigger
until the digit ticks to zero.

I like to iron a white shirt
on mornings I'm hungover.
Sometimes I button it right
to the neck, neat-like. Unsure
exactly what it is I'm meant
to ask forgiveness for,
I do so anyway, but also want
this loud unpleasant static
on the speakers as my coffin
penetrates the curtain,

just like when my mother's did.
My mother's mother (widowed
young, five kids) kept a dairy
herd and never said much. I never
knew a farmer who said much.
The earth has a kind of hard
muteness that will do that.
Sometimes I can barely
keep my mother shut.
I mean my mouth. My mother's

mother's father William Shannon
found a stranger on his doorstep
and learned he had three days to flee
before the farmhouse would be set
alight with all of them inside it.
And my mother's mother Martha,
her five sisters and six brothers,
and all the cattle and sheep
were herded on a chartered train
from Bantry to Cork to Armagh city.

My friend Bartek thinks only the Poles
should be allowed to write free verse
since they've watched their borders
shift so often, watched their homes
razed and then rebuilt them, watched
them burnt again and then rebuilt
them, and at some point you stop.
I know that every evil act I ever saw
committed had at its core
identity. When they exploded David

and our windows shook, that was
because of who he was, of what skin
he was born in. Ernie was on call
and among the first to reach the scene
and told me there was one torso
lodged in a tree, and it had not
been possible to identify them all,
and that's irony, I suppose,
and all that one can do is stop
the counter's roll at double zero.

AMY ACRE

Ice Baby

When I hear what is happening in America I turn back on myself,
crouch on the landing where no light falls and wait for the piglet
in her sniffle to unlung. Like I know the full farmyard of her
discontents and which corn snack to invoke against rainfall, I know
no bailiff is coming to box me in a van, god complex me from her.
No vested blizzard will surprise me on the dawn shift when I'm
slow-eyed and puttyesque. No fat-fisted plucker will pick her from
school for a fresh-painted purgatory to watch other kids crack,
gnawing on chalkends as twilight comes knocking, keeping her cry
for my step. I will not exchange my biography for the role of deterrent.
Her face will grace neither Twitter storm nor petition. She will not
be raised by ghosts and forget the arrangement of my voice.
Her fire will not be quashed under a bleeding flag but over there
they are freezing and the president is so afraid. Over there the children
are freezing, the mothers are freezing, the fathers are freezing,
the supply teachers, the accountants and Uber drivers and poets,
the potwashes and lawyers are freezing, the orphans and stepkids.
Their gloves have gone fuzzy, they are layering their tights and blowing
into each other's faces. They are drinking white spirit and weeping
into photographs. They are avalanche and they are the climbers
twitching under vast white rock and I look only long enough to
zip up her raincoat and remember this has nothing to do with us.

In the wet-aired trenches of the Tube I was

a tigress, cub in jaw, sniffing out cordite
and saltpetre, spying warshapes in the dark.
I saw the parched black mouth of the track,
a long, marauding animal, limbless slither,
crabapple on tongue. My child, months
from the womb, hung from my teeth.
I ferried her by the neck and saw her death
everywhere. I hung on the grit-kissed wall
until the train pummelled in to replace
imagination. Forgive me, I saw things
I couldn't tell my therapist. I mauled
thought to silence and counted my steps
and talked to myself in dissertation. I saw
others, smelt their milk in the slow lifts,
smiled at their litters and wondered if
they too saw their babies fall, if they fought
escalators tumbling with fear, if we were
all staring down the same muzzle, waiting
for the grip to drop from our own hands.

RICHARD O'BRIEN

Calcant

is a fancy word for bellows-treader
is a fancy word for a big fucker in the basement

sweating so the music plays
the edifice depending   not on angelic choirs

but on the motion of the burly man who steps
from plank to plank   a motion positively Sisyphean

is a fancy word for getting out of bed each day
to hoist a weight which never changes

see him grunt and bob beneath the strains
which summon in the boss's daughters'

weddings and his funeral   fugue
is a fancy word for how a trolley-car

of lumberjacky   beat Nordeasterners
can halfway sleep while bouncing up

East Hennepin before waking to do
it all again   to clatter down the steps

like some human   dumb waiter
to assume a crouch   primed on the blocks

that rough wood   that dark basement air
and step the air up   up into the pipes

which point shinily heavenward   to cascade
out from polished oak melodious   and free

is a fancy word for what spills out into the air
and not the gears which turn beneath it all

MAURICE RIORDAN

The Flaw

We each have our tragedy. Yours, she's telling me to my face,
is my fixation on the local. I nod.
(We are, after all, in The Pyrotechnists Arms).
You know what I mean! Those litanies of place names.
And besides you're stuck in some wormhole.
Band names. Brand names. Dead girlfriends.
You can only drink out of a straight pint glass.
You can only sleep on clean white sheets.
You boil pigs' feet and eat Golden Wonders in their skins.
Nothing's to your liking unless you had it moons ago.

It's true I like to sleep on freshly laundered linen.
Though one time, believe me, life was wild and scary.
I slept between menhirs high above the Atlantic.
On a Chesterfield in the penthouse of a Park Plaza.
I was on the lookout for my life's calling. A crusade.
I'd Africa in mind. Child poverty. River blindness.
The last surviving pair of Northern White Rhino.
I'd one foot on the gangplank of a boat bound for Mombasa.

O Brave New World that had such novels in it!
You sold out. You turned sour. You went to seed.
You've become this old gasser full of wind and sentiment.
Her index finger is prodding my ribcage.
Gently now, as though I'm an endangered species.
You're a throwback, a quisling, a swipe left, a a a
I'm nodding again. At everything she has to tell me.

The Shoulder Tap

Matty, in memory

I'm walking along the towpath though also
peering into the undergrowth it seems beside
the Leamlara (in Irish Léim Lárach, the Mare's Leap)
– a slur on, I'm thinking, the little river where
with the tip of a finger he's keeping my body afloat
until he laughs and seeing he's yards upstream
I go under kicking like a calf – that's to say
I'm years away when I hear the voice, soft and cajoling,
dwell on my name – then the tap on my shoulder.
And I swing in sudden anger to fuck at him.
The oldest trick in the book... and I've fallen for it.

ALICE MILLER

Seams

In time all cities blur and connect
as each street remembers
another, remembers the downward
pressure on your temple
as the plane rises, rises, as the lights
of one city are gurgled by fog, and what's left
is one more night between time zones.

What glow here. What unbreakable seams.

You know the earth, like your body, can't take this,
won't last, and yet tonight you need too much to get home.
What else do you need too much?
Another plane slips across darkness before the cloud shifts and again
a city – its networked wide grids, grips of colour, unreal green
of some outskirts' stadium before that black cloud pours back in.

Did you use your time on earth to save
what you wanted? Did you use anyone
the way you should? What song
will you sing as the light leaves,
as the mask's lowered over your eyes?

The Goddess of Death

There's a Māori legend they read to us as kids
about the trickster demigod Māui who decides to defeat death.
He hides from the goddess of death and while she sleeps
he crawls up inside her vagina
to kill her in her sleep.

He's about to become the man who defeats death forever
but instead, because of the chirrup
of a bird, the goddess wakes
and squeezes Māui
to death between her thighs.

You can see why the story stays with you.

Now I guess we're not only crawling up between her thighs
but we're bringing everything we can carry
driving up in our SUVs and our jetplanes
stuffing this woman's vulva full of metal, plastic,

space junk, Primark bikinis and polystyrene
mannequins, clipboards and laptops, parabens
and silicone, we're shoveling it all deep
in her bloodstream
while she tries to rest, as she's been trying to rest

all these years since Māui woke her.
Still, the stories say she created death.
We will never let her rest.

KATHRIN SCHMIDT
translated by Sue Vickerman

birdknacks

birds have got these world-counteracting smart-alec
knacks: techno-turbojet shoulders and hup...
they alone got plucked off lesbos on the salty
sea breeze, while the wingless and flightless were powerless,
even to get a mention in the press. feeling guilty
about my rightful guiltlessness, i ate nonetheless
and drank, played scrabble, slept in.
lesbos under a swollen, bloated sun –
i saw it chocabloc with sentry towers
and darkest depths. defensive, on the beach at usedom
i wore a total riot of bathing attire. swimming
in the sea. diving for mussels. lovely
way to spend time, i thought, as a breeze came up too
and massaged my skin. once dry i lounged later
on the beach, a hand across my eyes. unaltered
the swollen, bloated sun, lesbos just like over on usedom,
hi-tech birdflight between them.

*Usedom is a German holiday island destination that
was popular among working people in the former GDR*

amazonisch amazon

no sign of a seasonal dip in my bank account,
no lightning after the thunderbolt.
though meant to bust open that rotten barrel, it passed over
and went elsewhere. say no more. i won't waste words
that can move my mouth for things worthwhile. my house
is ever in the bank's stranglehold, never
will it let go. but my money, although hard done-to,
digs its honest furrow. fat chance greece will follow,
its debt grown way down below
its collar. if it crashes, you'll hear
how *the washington trumpet*'s herald of rage
blazes easterly over the atlantic. such harmony in the tunes
being played on all the various sides. how the drum
reverberates left for spite, right for incitement.
i hate the thought of importing cheap asians
to bottom this household's badly mopped-up
mess, and yet the amazon woman in me
battles for open borders,
speaks out, setting the *her* of herself aside.
i look back at her as she passes, hung
in the air, my animus.

THOMAS LYNCH

Yossef

Some days I wake up angry at everything –
the dreams, the voices, the cross-backed donkey,
the bulging, gravid girl, the cuckoldry,
the troth I pledged regardless: love's a yoke.
Life's a gibbet, time's a torment and a thorn:
I am an old man, and she is beautiful.
These dark-of-night, footsore, long haul journeys:
the occupier's tally and tax, this
murderous fiat. I'm too old for this.
I've got better things to do. To build,
to join. I make do, shelter and husband.
Give her her due, the child's a bright star –
graceful like her, her calm, those wellspring eyes.
The herdsmen were dumbstruck, the Levantines –
their camels and wariness. Perfumes and gold?
What's frankincense and myrrh to refugees?
Our lot's a scourge, the way a mystery.
Some days it's magic just to be alive.

CHERYL FOLLON

Apple

That guy with the strawberry blonde hair and twisted-up features
had a father with strawberry blonde hair and twisted-up features,
and *he* had a father with strawberry blonde hair and twisted-up features.
And all of this right back
to the time when they were an apple on a branch
getting plucked off by a caveman,
and his dog at the side turning up things with its nose.

Motorway

That guy thinks there's something wrong with his dog.
It barks at everything – pigeons, postmen, aircraft.
He takes it past the Pagazzi Lighting warehouse with all the lampshades
    in cellophane
and the dog barks and barks. He takes it to the motorway overpass
so they can watch the traffic thundering underneath:
that pink VW with the suede soft top,
that hearse with smoke coming out of it. The dog barks and barks and barks.
After a while they climb down and head home and en route
call in on that constant irritant his daughter.

SOUMYAROOP MAJUMDAR

Adda

In our pauses the trundle of lorries,
nightlong cavalcades
echoing between tarmac
and the mortar of overhang.

Halal, No Beef
nailed on the walls
of Haji Saheb. Splashed
bucketfuls dissolve
the day's muck,
seek out stray kebabs
from under counters,
all brought gushing onto
the pavement by a jhaadu's
scraped arc; the shutter
comes down on its own feet.

Swirled, the saccharine
milk and water take on
a slow russet. Fruit-stall by day,
the only one around that has seen
a change of hands. This is jugaad,
we agree, life as a portmanteau.

Fish truck: first sign of morning.
Meltwater collects in potholes through
the unloading; chappals spatter
mud onto calves, lungis at half-fold.

The driver lights up, hands cupped
against the bluster of a saloon
trailing Raftaar. Bitter,

brown-paper smoke of beedi,
steam of reboiled chaa
touching mahogany.

Alipore Zoo

Always the big cat enclosure first,
their moans swelling the bell curves
of our brags. Tigers – *drugged of course* –
stretched out on rocks across a moat:

meagre Lakshman rekha for
the two drunks with garlands, short work.
The pong of spoonbills, whisked by scamper.
A cockatoo on the mesh wiring

climbing beak-and-claw. Between
the drying wings of ibises
and Shah Rukh's open arms the bubbling
of a meme, and surely some usurper

now where the litigon would strain,
on his hind legs, towards the roof.
Other days, caught in the snarl of school
rush hour, a few minutes on the bridge,

a glimpse of the elephants and, once,
not too long ago, in a cage
a stone's throw from the gurdwara
at the Rashbehari crossing,

a sloth bear; backdrop of boxing ring
and soaped-up bathers at a public
tube well, he'd sit dribbling
fruit pap, accustomed to intrigue.

VICTORIA KENNEFICK

Open Your Mouth

As a toddler
      Krishna ate clay
          for fun,
               his worried mother
                    prying open his mouth
                         felt herself whirling in space, lost
                            inside that baby mouth
                    the whole universe,
              moving and unmoving creation.
          The earth, its mountains and oceans,
        moon and stars,
     planets and regions
and the child Krishna
      with his wide-open mouth
         and her kneeling
            before him, and within
     that mouth another
universe
      and within
         that mouth
            another
universe
      and within
         that mouth
            another
universe
      and within
         that mouth
            another.
Eat,
     he said, holding out

the mud
in his chubby hand,
and so on,
or we both starve.
She opened wide, kept
her tongue flat. The substance
was thick
and active.
She did not know
what she was
tasting,
she swallowed
and felt
full.

(M)eat

I sucked marrow from bones at dinner,
my father's face a bloody grin of pride. I ate liver in chunks
for breakfast, pink and firm, jewels to adorn my insides.
I gloried in the feel of flesh, the exertion of the chew.
Until, holding my mother's hand in the English Market,
I saw them – turkey chandeliers, plucked,
bruised purple eyelids dainty lightbulbs.
Their smell, fresh as the insides of my mouth.
Mother stroked my hair. *There, there.* I refused to eat
meat, became pillowy, meek. She hid muscle under mashed potato,
I tasted its tang in soup. *Eat up,* my parents said. I could not
swallow. My skin goose-pimple yellow, doctors drew blood
in tiny, regular sips. Teeth turned to glass and shattered
in my mouth. All I could taste was blood.

January

I have begun the purge.
Month of hunger,
raindrops fall
from window sills, ice
slithers in puddles,
the smoky breath of animals
greets the air. Morning's back
already broken, veins
obvious on everything.
Emptying myself
of all things ripe
and wanton, I am winter grass.
Observe me survive
as earth's shoulder blades
that jut, cut up the sky
that pushes down on all of us
as if it wants to die.
See, I am transparent
as sunrise.
Starving, I count
my bones as valuable.

DON PATERSON

The Way We Were

Having made the error of finally agreeing to lunch with L – what had it been,
    twenty-three years? –
let's say the horror was mutual. That's a lie. She was still beautiful. Her shock
was ill-disguised, though.
Thereafter I stayed home. God, what I'd give to be yesterday's man again!
I miss those long afternoons by the dead phone, with a martini that never
    seemed to shrink.
I told Jarvis that I should not be disturbed, retreated to my den, hooked the
    shutters
and took up my station on what my wife used to call "the loser's couch", the
    one with the built-in surround,
before she left with the dogs. I loaded up a bunch of psychogram loops,
    turned on the wallscreen
and settled back. Initially, I confess, mostly with my pants round my knees,
    watching old drunken one-night stands
or those first dates when the two of you, still strangers, went further than
    you'd ever dare again.
Goddamn who *was* that handsome young buck? Though I worried about
    ageing even then.

Mostly the loops ran in 16k, and some had enough 3D data to frontform VR so
    I could watch them with the headset.
So much to see that I missed at the time: the couple fighting over money in
    the corner,
the wood pigeon on the branch outside the bedroom, the flailing elm in the
    window in the 8-ball.
And I could wind back as far as I liked: I recall when I was imaged last year,
    the mnemographer
remarked on what must have been the generally rapt quality of my attention,
as if I'd known the day would come when I'd be doing nothing else.

Anyone using the phrase "making memories" unironically should be shot in
    the head
unless they only have a year to live, and their kids are very young. Still, I was
    glad I had.
I blew the last cheque from the streaming revenue for *Half-Lives* on Jarvis's
    severance,
a year's-worth of IV nutro I could just piss back out, and three new modules
    for my Mnemosync
that would allow me a) to re-render the loops as first person (our memories are
    all of someone else)
b) to sub out my kainotype for my paleotype and c) to implant active AI into up
    to five simultaneous agents
within any given scene. Armed with all this, I could insert my waking self
    directly back into those bright vignettes
which I could not only play and replay forever, but live within, as in a lucid
    dream.

I should probably mention at this point that I was always an earlier adopter.
The guy a bit too keen to download the beta, or camping on the sidewalk to be
    first in line
for his half-working piece of shiny crap. I guess I love the future. It holds such
    promise!
It just always turns up a bit too early, a bit too good to be true. A failure at the
    lab to calibrate the self-imaging algo
meant that the star of my home movies kept flicking between then-me and
    now-me,
leaving me in a narcoplegic lock until it self-corrected. Because I could now
    only see myself from the inside out,
the effect was initially comic: me, stuck on the park slide, with the parents
    yelling *Get that old wino off there*
or my liver-spotted hand up in the air, proudly answering a times table quiz for
    Mrs Garland.
Others were just depressing. That day at the lido with Mum and Dad, thirty
    years older than them both,

the two of them trying to locate a facial expression of tender revulsion, and
     failing, and failing;
or that first kiss with L – at the hedge behind her house, and her – sixteen, like
     apple blossom,
her mouth pliant and cool with cheap white wine – springing back in horror at
     the whitebeard with the loose teeth
and the tongue down her throat. Worse was looking down at our naked bodies,
     latched like some sick white crab
praying she wouldn't open her eyes before I could waken my hand on the
     escape key.

Yet I am already looking back on these as the best of times, as for days now
I've been locked in a two-second glitch-loop, where I am stuck with my mouth
     on the full breast
of my young beautiful mother, who looks down at me and will not stop
     screaming and screaming.

PENNY NEWELL

speaking because of bodies

because they wr over-using their knees and openly
expressing their inadequate height and miscalculations
each felt compelled by these efforts
to share a weakening story about their body.

when i was a young man my left testicle twisted
and now he has jst the one real testicle he tells them
and now when he's fcking a woman the other retracts
into his body, crops up somewhere-else a rubber hernia
which he thumbs down whn her back is turned.

when i was a child i trapped this finger in a car door
do you see how short it is, its a ten year old finger
nt literally, but that's how she feels when she looks at it
she remembers it contused and screaming wonders
how do parts of the body story intensities of pain?

when i was a child i trapped a cat that was deaf
in a wicker laundry basket it was so cruel
imagine the fear of that cat in the dark and silence
she is aware it's not obviously a story about the body
so she describes the guilt that made her spiritual
like nothing else before or after, indescribable really.

in the breaks they listned to the wind in the high heather
each person was so obviously thinking about hauntings
that when it came down to it, they had shared so very little.

ANNE BARNGROVER

A lot of stuff happened, and I quit being normal

Meme from the anime Boogiepop and Others

No one can reach me when my hormones spike. I go off
to live in a forest of bird's nest ferns. People are aggressive
that I am not special. What I'm feeling is a condition
of being human. I guess everyone thinks they're dying
all the time and daydreams about getting in front of death
so they don't have to worry about it anymore. Cool!
She has endured a series of catastrophic events. If someone
complains that a book made them depressed, I'll read it.
When I have a day off, my mind decides to pretend
I'm itching and burning just so it has something to do.
My endocrinologist says I'm sensitive. My dentist says
I'm sensitive. My gynecologist says I'm sensitive.
My allergist says I'm sensitive. My therapist says I'm so
sensitive, she has to reorganize our healing schedule.
When I get acupuncture, the needles keep popping
out of my earlobes. That's supposed to mean anxiety.
An essay someone else wrote about my ex went viral,
but people assumed I'd been dramatic for seven years.
Why is my bird's nest fern dying now? I kind of enjoyed
the MRI. Like a rollercoaster through a cave, snuggled
in tight like a boxed cigar. They were looking at the center
of my brain, seed mushed inside a pumpkin's wet head.
Excess cells have a great time sloughing off hormones
to convince me that I'm dying. Literal symptom: *sensation
of impending doom.* Fear *backed and packed* like fish irises
in that Elizabeth Bishop poem. I feel safe when I hear
a really accurate description. How can people be left
and just continue living? Reading my tarot cards,
I keep turning up stars and swords. Reading my coffee
dregs, all I can see is water. *Where are you going after this?*
The medication shadows my vision for about four

to five minutes after lying down. I chill on the couch
and wait for it to return. Sometimes, all I can see
is a black orb in front of my eyes. *That goes away
for most patients over time.* Last summer, I wanted to feel
bad enough so people would believe me. I spilled coffee
on my laptop and lost a thirteen-page essay. I know
I'm going to receive a lecture, but I don't trust whatever's
in the Cloud. I wrote my essay back from memory
on printer paper in the mall Starbucks before my turn
at the Apple store. I wrote enfolded by glass sunlight
and giant ferns. Sometimes, there's no one who can see
anything real about me. I wrote it back word for word.

Wum Town
*A collaboration between Liz Berry
and Black Country photographer
Tom Hicks*

LIZ BERRY

Yam Yam's Diner

Somewhere, beyond all this,
I'm elbows down on the counter in Yam Yam's Diner,
sunflower oil slicking my ponytail,
ruby t-shirt, blue apron,
Our Lady of Perpetual Succour,
all a hardworking man might stoop
to kiss the knuckles of,
stagger out in the diesel-yellow morning
yearning to taste;
serving a little *chick* and *bab*,
tea slurry with sugar, bacon
with a sly crisp of skin, bread thick
as a dictionary flipped to the entry:
clammed to jeth.
I'd love them, the men,
in their overalls and boots
you could stamp on the toes of;
the tired ones, the trodden, the young,
their chins still soft with bum-fluff.
I'd hold their dreams
– so tenderly – understanding
that there is no heaven but this:
a grease-spangled Portakabin, the rhyme
the body yields when it's finally full.
So get it while you can;
by three I'll be gone,
tables wiped, shutters down,
already feeling the afternoon sun
on that soft bare spot on my nape,
the scent of fat and salt swinging like incense
as I pull out the pins
and let loose my hair.

The Dereliction

Love me like that pub on Darkhouse Lane,
sweetheart of wet-the-beds and creeping rot.

Love me like I have no windows, no doors, just wild
blue streaming through unarrested.

Love me to the bare bones, through rain and rough weather,
time singing its song of *dereliction dereliction.*

Touch your palms to my walls, their yielding brick,
and remember how my face held its look

of abandon, how young we were, my white dress lifted
and blown reckless as a kite in a storm.

Blue Heaven

Our poem which art in blue heaven,
give us this morning,
daffodils spilling spring's song like yolk,
moss sporing on the guttering, snug
for wet-the-beds; jenny-wren and weeping birch
watching over us, our unanswered emails
and half-built Lego palaces, milk cups
and toast crumbs, photographs of us
in the nineties, drunk and so in love
we look like children.
Give us griefs and small kindnesses,
wunce apon a time in clumsy boy's hand
on the back of a phone bill,
library books and Germolene, sanitary towels
soaked with clotted rubies,
pyjamas shed beneath the bunk beds
like adder skins, money spiders, stories,
the nights we touch in darkness
with that wild honeymilk of recognition.
Tenderise our hearts to all that is holy:
the dog and her blanket, the playgroup collage,
and forgive us our trespasses –
pulling tight the shutters on our hearts
when others are knocking,
cussing in the night when we stumble to the cot.
Teach us to love each other as the tree loves the rain,
never wasting a drop.

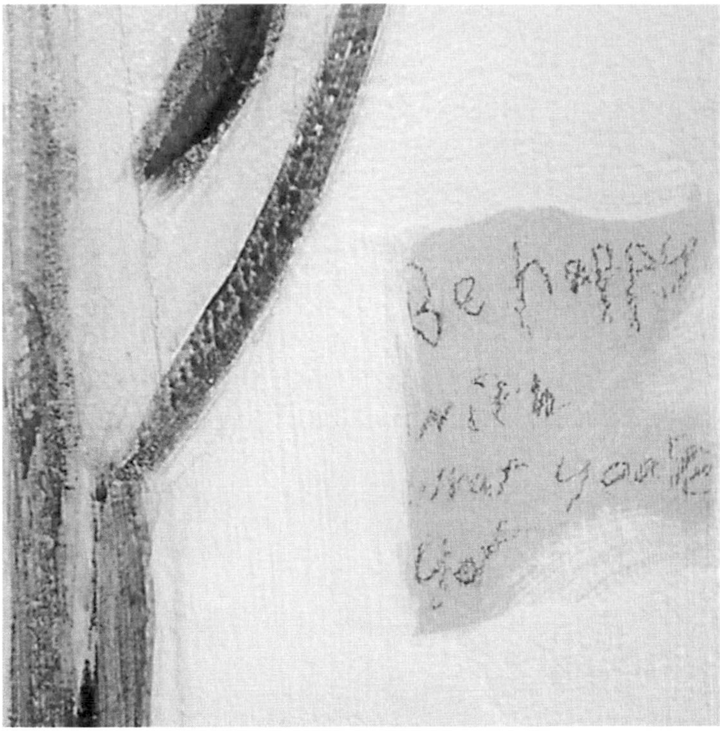
Be happy

Essay

LISTEN EVERYBODY: ON DENISE RILEY

Maria Johnston

To hold a true note could be everything

('An Awkward Lyric')

"It is a book about listening closely (to oneself and others)", Emily Berry discerns of *Time Lived, Without Its Flow* (Picador, 2019) on the flyleaf of this new edition of Denise Riley's riveting essay on maternal loss and arrested time. First published in 2012 by Capsule Press, the essay, written in the aftermath of the sudden death of Riley's adult son Jacob in 2008, is composed of notes painstakingly etched at intervals (two weeks, one month, five months, and so on) after the event, all of which, as Riley states in a short prefatory section, "can walk around only the rim of this experience". These are followed by a longer 'Postscript' written at a further distance of three years from the time of death that loops back to consider, and communicate in a more studied way, what the poet has "had to learn about living in arrested time". "I'll not be writing about death, but about an altered condition of life", the essay opens as Riley – poet, philosopher, teacher – sets out to harness in language "this curious sense of being pulled right outside of time, as if beached in a clear light".

"But how could such a striking condition ever be voiced?" Riley enquires. The answer seemed to necessitate two different forms: the direct, prose response that is *Time Lived, Without its Flow* and what might be termed its oblique, indirect counterpart in poetry, 'A Part Song', published first in the *London Review of Books* in 2012 (accompanied by a podcast of Riley reading the poem) and then as the restive focal-point of Riley's 2016 collection *Say Something Back*. Nominated as that collection was for various high-profile poetry prizes, accounts of Riley's career to date focus on this moment as a defining one which took her from relative obscurity into the light of the poetry mainstream. Her influence on and importance to the brightest poets and critics writing today – one thinks of Frances Leviston, Sarah Howe, Ailbhe Darcy, Leontia Flynn and Berry herself – is increasingly audible and this new edition of *Time Lived, Without Its Flow* comes to us along with a new and heftier *Selected Poems* (which presents *Say Something Back* in its entirety and offers generous selections from Riley's earlier work). The essay is prefaced with an introduction by Max Porter, author of the acclaimed *Grief is the Thing with Feathers* (Faber, 2015), who has also taken part in a public conversation with Riley and Emily Berry at the London Review Bookshop.

Another recent interview with Berry for The Poetry Society had Riley remark on how the "tension between exposure and the wish not to be seen at all" is "held especially sharply" by the lyric poem. Reading this new edition of *Time Lived, Without its Flow*, and tuning in to the publicity and promo-work that goes with its high-profile republication, one might begin to feel that one is getting to know the 'real' Denise Riley in an intimate way. As Porter himself notes in his introduction: "her asking is so deftly personal, and so clear, it reminds me [...] of my mum". How then does the private lyric poet take on her own grief in such a public way without coming up against charges of egotism? 'Let no air now be sung' is the title of a poem from Riley's *Say Something Back* which seems to echo the voice of 'Music' in Monteverdi's *Orfeo*, and how can one sing one's own suffering, especially when, as Riley the theorist and philosopher knows, there can be an "ostentatious aspect to self-portrayal"? How can she achieve in poetry the "fragile balance", as she put it in a 1995 interview, that is: "to use the stuff of your life while refusing to shine as the guiding light of it"?

In order to set the poems of Friedrich Rückert to music to compose his song cycle 'Kindertotenlieder' ('Songs on the Death of Children') Gustav Mahler explained: "I put myself in the position as though a child of mine had died; when I actually lost my daughter, I could no longer have written the songs." Riley is a poet who has always been able to inhabit imaginatively conditions of being and of feeling that are not her own and to make her 'I' merge with another's, through keen, empathetic attentiveness. Listening to her perform her revelatory collage poem 'Letters from Palmer' (from 1993's *Mop Mop Georgette*) recently, I marvelled anew at the way she distils the poem out of letters written by the artist and engraver Samuel Palmer, working isolate phrases in lapidary fashion through a visual and musical technique that sets them at angles to each other, making them catch the light to communicate their truths in a symphonic way. This time round, however, reading it as part of this new *Selected Poems*, I was brought up short by the phrase "*Writhing* for the death of my son" – and struck by how we cannot now read or hear these lines – and in particular that italicised word "Writhing", so close to the word and act of 'writing' – without thinking of the death of Riley's own son and her writing of and through that loss. The original expression in Palmer's letter is wordier: "What should I do without resources, writhing, as I have been now for three years, in agony for the death of my son, full of promise, and just going to Oxford?" Riley's edit, cutting away the padding on either side, makes the wrenching admission more forceful and astonishing.

Such a technique chimes with the ways in which Riley's recent work comprises a rebuke against the kind of 'Death Lit' that ends with an exhortation to 'move on' (narratives that Riley, speaking at the London Review Bookshop, has deemed "radically misconceived and cruel"). As readers of Palmer's *Life and Letters* will know, the artist's refusal to conform his grief in the years after this son's death prompted his surviving son, editing his work posthumously, to offer an "explanation" to readers over fears about what would be perceived as his grieving father's "apparent want of self-control". Riley's orchestration of phrases from Palmer's letters not only releases the latent poetry in his sensitive, tactile and alert observations of the world around him (and his own visionary art has clearly influenced her own), but comprises a necessary humane intervention to become a searing poetic synthesis of what it is to make art in the face of loss and go on attending to the intricacies of light, sub-light and colour that survive intractable difficulty and colourless petrification: "O the playful heave and tumble of lines in the hills here. / We are first green and then grey and then nothing in this world" ('Letters from Palmer').

"She's someone who touches on quite extreme and almost unpalatable emotion, and she is also very good on time, on this strange temporality of emotional states – or on shock, or the fall of the light, or a gesture, it's often some vivid arrested quality that her writing enacts", Riley described Emily Dickinson in a 2015 interview, and Kenneth Koch's description of Dickinson's poetry as "high explosives hidden in small, neat boxes" could be applied to many of Riley's poems also. "Vocabularies have been invented to describe her style of thinking", Helen Vendler has written of Dickinson and the tumults of the mind as well as of the heart are what Riley as poet-philosopher dramatises in her work. Indeed, far from being diminished by death, one feels more than anything in the 'Postscript' section of *Time Lived, Without its Flow*, the life of a mind, probing and muscular, at work. With that forensic alertness that is uniquely hers, Riley contemplates the workings of sound in poetry and the relation between time and language. "For the radical stasis of time, one decisive note is Emily Dickinson's in about 1864", Riley elucidates Dickinson's poem 'I felt a Cleaving in my Mind –' attending closely to the word "Sound" ("But Sequence ravelled out of Sound – / Like Balls – upon a Floor –") and how its "intense resonances" work: "sound is sustained on the ear by its repetition, and by the expectation that another sound will follow on [...] if sequence were truly to fall apart from sound, then the hearer could no longer expect any future unrolling, or could [no longer] discern any principle of successive sounding". For Vendler, Dickinson's image suggests: "the notes of a musical score which are disarticulating themselves and forming a dissonant heap". "Words move, music moves / Only in time", T.S. Eliot intoned, but what happens when time has become suspended for the poet? Unlike narrative prose, "a poem may be carried by oscillation, a to-and-fro, rather than by some forward-leaning chronological drive", Riley eloquently surmises thereby opening up poetry to "an experience of time that is not linear" and that may perhaps be analogous to the art of song.

In 'Following Heine' from *Say Something Back* Riley reworks Heinrich Heine's poem 'Ich hab' im Traum geweinet' ('I cried in a dream') into an unsparing new form, doing away with the three regular four-line stanzas of the original and compressing it into a shape that, refusing any breath between the lines, makes for a single, unalleviated vocalisation that forbids progress through the repetition of its key motifs (crying, dreaming, waking), and has an immensity of silence pressing in on and around it:

I cried in my sleep as I thought
you were in your grave, I woke but
went on weeping. I dreamt you'd
abandoned me, I woke to cry bitterly.
I slept. In my sleep, I wept as I
dreamt you were still good to me.
I awoke in unrelenting tears.

Of course this poem in Heine's German (along with others from his 'Lyrisches Intermezzo') really began its life when composer Robert Schumann set it to music for his song cycle 'Dichterliebe' ('A Poet's Love') in 1840. Universally regarded as the most emotionally intense of the songs with its unusually exposed vocal line, minor sonority and unsettling, dissonant duality between voice and piano, 'Ich hab' im Traum geweinet' is striking for the way that it articulates stasis and silence while also dissolving any clear-cut distinction between dream, memory and reality. Commenting on what it is like to perform Schumann's 'Dichterliebe' the tenor James Gilchrist singles this song out for its gaps and silences: "The score is so full of empty space. It's really arresting and quite unnerving". As Charles Rosen has interpreted it: "Future and present are almost unreal: only the past within the present has any force. Illusion and memory act with a power that makes them indistinguishable from reality. The illusion explodes however: the singer cannot finish the song. [...] This is perhaps the first piece of music in which empty silence plays a role as great or even greater than that of the notes". From this account alone one can see how Riley would be drawn to such a cast of mind-out-of-time; as an articulation of the arrested and otherworldly atemporality of grief that eludes narrative rendering, it comes close to perfect.

"I suppose I've got an obstinate attachment to musicality (and 'musicality' is a vague word, as is 'cadence'). If I entitle things 'Lyric' it's because the main property that I've aimed at in those poems is some musical brightness", Riley revealed in a 1995 interview with Ramona Huk. However, Riley's is not empty euphony or a decorative music. Schumann believed music to be the "highest potential of poetry" and Riley's compelling musicality – stemming from her lifelong interest in hymns and the "harsh musicality" of the border ballad tradition – is what any reader entering her poetry (both its small chamber works and the more expansive concert-hall pieces) will feel most strongly. Indeed, as one reads

Selected Poems, one builds an extensive playlist of all of the vocal music that hums within the pages. "And you're not listening to a word I say", is the final rebuke (taken from the pop song 'It's in His Kiss') of the gloriously synaesthetic tapestry '*Lure 1963*' (in *Mop Mop Georgette*). Crowded with voices, 'A Misremembered Lyric' implicates misquoted fragments from 'Something's Gotten Hold of My Heart', 'Rhythm of the Rain' and the Two Gilberts' music hall number 'Do Shrimps Make Good Mothers?' into its shifting, disconsolate intertextual weave. In 'Shantung' we have not only Marvin Gaye asking 'Can I get a witness' (his "Listen everybody" misquoted here as "Come on everybody") but the *EastEnders* theme song ('Anyone Can Fall in Love') as sung by Anita Dobson in her role as the tragic Angie. The track list is endless, making for a dizzying soundscape of voices in performance and haunting layers of clashing intertextual echoes. As Riley has written in an essay on her "unresolved" poem, 'The Castalian Spring': "I append my signature sheepishly because I know I am a sounding chamber in poetry, even more so than in prose, since more than the content of the poem is derived". Like the figure of Echo, lyric poetry is, as Riley has identified, "driven by rhyme, condemned to repetition of the cadences and sound associations of others' utterances".

Are all of these misremembered lyrics and dismembered lyrics an attempt at a unique, personal voice or are they a strategy for occluding any autobiographical utterances that might be sourced to the poet herself? What's interesting is how Riley so often chooses song lyrics from songs that have been recorded over time by many artists, the 'cover version' supplementing the original, making these songs the property of many singers or, ultimately, of none. There is no 'original' voice left as a range of interpretations co-exist. For instance, 'Something's Gotten Hold of My Heart' has been covered by artists including Nick Cave, another innovator of the (murder) ballad tradition, and Robson and Jerome, while 'The Unquiet Grave' of the quivering coda of her multivoiced elegy 'A Part Song' exists in versions by Joan Baez and Luke Kelly among others. In this endlessly sounding (there is no full stop) extended cadence in which the dead boy, undergoing apotheosis, upholds his own condition of being, I also hear on the "fretful wave" Ralph Vaughan Williams' part-song 'Full Fathom Five' from his 'Three Shakespeare Songs'. Riley's use of song is complex and far-reaching. By incorporating song lyrics into her work and passing these human voices in their all-too-human performances through the distortions and amplifications of the poetic process, Riley is adding another layer to the recording history of these songs, composing them into something rich, strange and infinitely variable, but the ghosts of all of these performers, these voices we believe in – whose words and feeling we take to be true at particular points in our lives – linger on there too. Her poetry therefore becomes a vibrant and vibrating texture of voices shimmering through various tricks of tonal and timbral manipulation.

The way that music is used in film must also be of interest to Riley. In the poem 'Little Eva' from *Say Something Back*, lyrics taken from Eva Boyd's hit song 'The Loco-Motion' (as Riley establishes in a note to the poem) appear in animated italics:

> Time took your love – now time will take its time.
> 'Move on', you hear, but to what howling emptiness?
> The kinder place is closest to your dead
> where you lounge in confident no-motion, no thought
> of budging. Constant in analytic sorrow, you abide.
> *It even makes you happy when you're feeling blue.*
> *Jump up, jump back.* Flail on the spot.
> I can disprove this 'moving on' nostrum.
> *Do the loco-motion in my living room.*

The poem opens with a deadlocked, incontrovertible statement about "time", that repeats the word (three times) to deadening effect (that mid-line Dickinsonian dash effectively stopping time) like a spell of petrification that calls out to be sung as incantation. That, along with the exhortation to "move on" (already mentioned in relation to Riley's resistance to simplified narratives of grief as a tabulated process) might bring us back to Eliot's formulation, but poetic tradition and the moribund poetic dead are soon drowned out by other voices. Although it's not referenced, there may also be a snatch of the song 'Girl of Constant Sorrow' in that line about being "constant in analytic sorrow" as well as a faint echo of the hymn 'Abide with Me' as Merleau-Ponty cites Heidegger from *Time Lived, Without its Flow*: "I am myself time, a time which 'abides' and does not flow or change". Like Schumann with his blue flower, Riley's synaesthetic imagination is charged by the colour blue – so many of the songs she broadcasts in her own lyrics mention blue as a colour or feeling – and here it is the song and dance 'The Loco-Motion' (a 1962 hit for Boyd, since when it has been covered by Kylie Minogue and Atomic Kitten among others) that blasts from the past into the poem's boxy space with its irresistible call to get up and move like a locomotive.

However, what might seem like nostalgic or ironic reference to a boppy innocuous pop song takes on a deeply unsettling glow when we remember that song and its choreography in the terrifying context of a scene in David Lynch's 2006 film *Inland Empire* in which a group of Valley girls do 'The Loco-Motion' in the living room of the main character Nikki Grace / Susan Blue (played by Laura Dern) only to then vanish completely, leaving the room howlingly empty as the music cuts and the sequence breaks. The effect is shocking in the extreme as the welcome comfort of a recognisable song and dance number is abruptly pulled away. Described by Roger Ebert as a film that "continually readjusts perceptions of time", *Inland Empire* foregrounds discontinuity and the experience of existing out of time not merely through the plot (which defies any realistic narrative logic), but the filming technique itself. Interviewed after the film's release, Laura Dern constantly employed the phrase "in the moment" to describe the experience of shooting *Inland Empire*; because of the deliberate absence of a script, such a lack of foreknowledge left her free to be whatever self was in that moment with no sense of futurity. The fact that the film was shot by a single handheld camera intensified the experience and all of this to me resonates with a passage from *Time Lived, Without Its Flow* in which Riley, noting how "any attempt at descriptive writing soon reaches an impasse [...] A life of no time cannot be recounted", turns to cinema instead for an analogy: "Maybe only the cinema could show it. Not by means of any cinematic plot, certainly, but through the camerawork itself".

The disorienting, non-linear quality of Lynch's films seems to me helpful in entering and inhabiting the similarly disconcerting spaces of Riley's poems, insofar as they allow themselves to be inhabited, but so too is Lynch's designed use of music in his work and, specifically, his exploitation of the relation between performance and illusion. Who can forget the impact of the scene in Lynch's *Mulholland Drive* in which Rebekah Del Rio sings a version of Roy Orbison's 'Crying' in Spanish ('Llorando') at the Silencio Club in a performance so emotive that it moves the two central characters to tears and to reach out to each other for consolation. The singer's performance is pure make-believe: that Del Rio is lip-syncing becomes obvious as, just as the song reaches climax, she falls to the floor even as the song keeps playing. This, as it turns out, is a pre-recorded track and only the presence of her body may be taken as 'real'. But does this make the emotion felt or the experience itself any less real? It means that illusion and artifice are part of art, but it also means, and this is key to Riley's work, that the relation between singer and song is not at all a matter of straightforward, unmediated autobiography, of personal emotion or experience being expressed in words. Song, in Riley's poetic manipulations, creates the distance between the 'I' of the poem and its audience even as it draws the reader-as-listener in to share in the emotive moment. For a poet whose work so often refers to masks, mascara, make-up and forms of concealment, nothing can be taken at face value, it all happens at the level of the heart and its "atrocious beat".

"My proffered self is always something of a dislocated 'I' – recalling the protagonist of Beckett's monologue who speaks in stage blackness, her face reduced to a mouthing pair of shrouded lips, her name simply 'Mouth'", Riley disclosed in *The Words of Selves* (2000). Even with the fact of her grief as laid out in *Time Lived, Without its Flow*, we know that, in *Say Something Back* as elsewhere we cannot expect any straightforward relation between the 'I' of these poems and the 'I' of Denise Riley. "She do the bereaved in different voices", the performer of the staggering elegy 'A Part Song' riffs on Eliot at one point, more in tune with Jessye Norman singing all four roles of Schubert's 'Der Erlkönig' than with the ordinary, bereaved mother who sits before an audience in London speaking about loss. The poet is more than one thing, and plays many parts, just as we ourselves are. Truth, varnished, comes to us through shades and silences, through echo and indirection: the composed artifice of poetic form with its endless reverberations, recapitulations, cover versions and versions of recovery, is finally the only frame that we can trust.

Perhaps that, in the end, is why these two books need to exist alongside each other: the prose describes and pinpoints, confident of a readership, of its own futurity, of its potential to console, while the poetry sends us spinning, burns holes in the fabric, hauls the reader in to attend to strophe and catastrophe, doubt and dissonance, as a range of alternating voices sound their own persistent erasure across time and space. "I work to earth my heart" is the ambiguous line from *Time Lived, Without its Flow* that adorns the back cover of the new edition and, much like Dickinson's "ravel" and "cleave", that verb "to earth" can mean a variety of things at once: to bury, to hide or conceal, but also "to connect to reality, to ground in authentic experience". Ultimately, the disquieting tension between lyre and liar is at the heart of Riley's flickering vocal arrangements across lines that, though only "made of words" (to quote W.S. Graham), catch us along even as they keep us at bay: that insist on empathy, on the communality of art and on the force of make-believe, that know, as Riley herself has remarked, that "we are human and nothing human is strange to us" and yet that we are strangers to ourselves, here one minute, gone the next. "What we want from a poem is not ultimately a message, a story, a graspable or paraphraseable content of some kind but rather an invitation to listen, and to listen again", Angela Leighton has opined. With the publication of these two indispensable volumes by Denise Riley – both of which, crucially, also exist in audiobook form – we get to do just that.

Essay

BORING AUDEN

Jeremy Noel-Tod

A re we bored of W.H. Auden? As Auden himself said, to ask the hard question is simple – and the answer to this one almost certainly depends on who 'we' are. For readers of my generation (b. 1978) Wystan Hugh Auden (1907–1973) was definitely still a Big Poet; and the further one went back in the twentieth century, the larger he loomed. "God, god, the stature of the man", wrote Sylvia Plath in her journal from 1953; Derek Walcott read Auden during his teenage years in 1940s St Lucia, finding him "far more adventurous" than Eliot or Pound; and the critic Richard Hoggart, who was ten years old when Auden published his first pamphlet, *Poems* (1928), wrote:

> Many of us who began our adult reading during the Thirties in England will always think of W.H. Auden with a particular warmth, with the family sense we reserve for those writers who place their fingers on the pulse of a crucial period.

For young English literary types between the wars, Thirties Auden was the Eighties Morrissey of his day: a not-obviously-heterosexual, charismatic loner who applied his wit to a wounded post-industrial landscape (Auden poem or Smiths lyric? "Where the Sunday lads come talking motor-bicycle and girl, / Smoking cigarettes in chains until their heads are in a whirl"). The remarkable thing is that Auden managed to repeat this trick with readers long after his first fame. When his cabaret song 'Funeral Blues' ("Stop all the clocks, cut off the telephone") was chosen by screenwriter Richard Curtis as the funeral reading in *Four Weddings and a Funeral* (1994), it prompted his publisher, Faber, to produce a short selection of his love poems that sold over a quarter of a million copies. The context of the film was important – John Hannah reads the lyric in memory of his older lover, played by Simon Callow – as was Auden's reputation as a gay poet, retrospectively acknowledged. James Fenton, one of the many twentieth-century poets whose work is unimaginable without Auden's example, remarked at the time: "A large number of people, since the AIDS epidemic, have become familiar with the experience of funerals at which a devastated boyfriend has to pay tribute to his prematurely dead lover. [...] The emotional scene [...] gains force from those memories".

Ian Sansom's rattlingly irreverent confession of his own fascination with Auden, *September 1, 1939: A Biography of a Poem* (4th Estate), circles around this afterlife. Its starting point is the poem that made Auden famous all over again in the twenty-first century, following the World Trade Center attacks in New York on September 11th, 2001:

I sit in one of the dives
On Fifty-Second Street
Uncertain and afraid
As the clever hopes expire
Of a low dishonest decade:
Waves of anger and fear
Circulate over the bright
And darkened lands of the earth,
Obsessing our private lives;
The unmentionable odour of death
Offends the September night.

Auden had only recently arrived in America from England, and these opening lines were written in response to the outbreak of war in Europe. After 9/11, they spoke so directly to the shock people felt following the

W.H. Auden by Cecil Beaton © The Cecil Beaton Studio Archive at Sotheby's

collapse of the Twin Towers that the poem began to circulate via the pre-Facebook agora of email lists (the fact that it was written in 9 stanzas of 11 lines each also acquired a Nostradamic significance).

For all its resonance, though, 'September 1, 1939' is among the chief exhibits that come to mind when I think of the Boring Auden. One reason he left England was to escape the expectation that a famous poet should be a public figure in wartime; as Paul Muldoon imagined it, in a dramatic monologue from *Meeting the British* (1987), "Wystan" did not want to be asked to "somehow inflate / myself and float // above their factories and pylons / like a flat-footed barrage balloon". But the temptation to make a speech from the other side of the Atlantic was strong. Auden later notoriously included 'September 1, 1939' among the "dishonest, or bad-mannered, or boring" pieces excluded from his *Collected Shorter Poems* (1966), and told an interviewer in 1972 that it was his "least favourite Auden poem", having scratched it in protest at the mendacity of its most famous line, "We must love one another or die". Taking it stanza by stanza, Sansom concurs that Auden's "grand gesturing [...] will eventually rather spoil and overwhelm" it, with lines that are "banal, deficient and silly". Yet he also tells us that he has been trying to write a book about Auden for twenty-five years.

Did Auden become boring over that quarter of a century? Sansom doesn't say so: for all its unvarnished criticism, his study is still a love letter, which begins with the word 'WOW' and answers the question "Will Auden last?" with the statement: "Auden has already lasted". Twenty-five years ago, the young poets of Sansom's generation shared this view. In the 'New Generation Special Issue' of *Poetry Review* from 1994, twenty poets were asked to name the modern poetry books that had influenced them most. Simon Armitage chose Auden's *Collected Poems*; Glyn Maxwell chose Auden's *Selected Poems*. Shortly afterwards, they were commissioned by the BBC to go to Iceland together, a trip that resulted in a sequel to Auden's poetic travel book with Louis MacNeice, *Letters from Iceland* (1937).

To a teenage Armitage-Maxwell fan, *Moon Country: Further Reports from Iceland* (1996) was an exciting volume: it was the first time I remember seeing poets report back from the real world. It was fresh, funny, formally various, and full of the pleasures of their early work. Read now alongside the original, though, *Moon Country's* version of the 'real world' feels mild and mini-breakish: Audenesque in voice but not vision. When Auden wrote in 'Journey to Iceland', "Europe is absent. This is an island and therefore / Unreal", he did so as someone who would, like other left-wing writers of his generation, travel to the Spanish Civil War (he drove an ambulance). *Moon Country*, by contrast, is a classic of mid-nineties End-of-History literature, when it sometimes seemed the only political question left in Britpop Britain was whether working-class blokes (Oasis/Armitage) and middle-class blokes (Blur/Maxwell) could get along.

This is a question that Sansom – the first from his family to go to university – makes a trenchantly personal aspect of his response to the "pitch and tone of Auden's work: it is definitely the poetry of someone who went to college". Auden's own self-conscious instability of tone, however, also produced his best poetry. The laughter-free zone that was F.R. Leavis accidentally nailed it when, attempting to patronise, he wrote: "Mr Auden's honesty there is no need to question; it may perhaps be said to manifest itself in the openness with which his poetry admits that it doesn't know how serious it supposes itself to be".

The need to be serious with intent is the demand of critics uncomfortable with wild irony. Thanks to them the most boring line in all of Auden, now, is "poetry makes nothing happen". If I never read another donnish discussion of how he did/didn't mean it, it will be too soon. The poem from which the line comes, 'In Memory of W.B. Yeats' ("Earth, receive an honoured guest / William Yeats is laid to rest"), is also due a moratorium, having inspired the worst 'speaking-as-a-craftsman' lines that Seamus Heaney ever turned, in his 1996 elegy for Joseph Brodksy: "Joseph, yes, you know the beat, / Wystan Auden's metric feet" ('Audenesque'). The evaluation of Yeats that really gets to the heart of Auden's genius in that poem comes a few lines earlier: "You were silly like us". I once read a parody that tweaked this into a couplet simply by adding a line break after "silly", then "..., Willy" at the end, and I now find it hard to remember this is not the original version. Perhaps the unhappy thought that Auden might be boring makes me willing to think him sillier than he was.

Auden liked to tease the liberal aesthetes of academia, writing in his early sixties essay 'The Poet and the City' that "a society which was like a really good poem" would be a fascist dystopia, while "vice versa, a poem which was really like a political democracy [...] would be formless, windy, banal and utterly boring". Nevertheless, it sometimes seems that the most daring post-Auden poets have taken up the challenge to sail close to the windy, as he himself did in later poems such as 'In Praise of Limestone' (1948), with its camply intimate evocation of post-Mussolini Italy: "They were right, my dear, all those voices were right / And still are; this land is not the sweet home that it looks".

J.H. Prynne, for example, burlesques the famous line from 'September 1, 1939' in one of his satirical Marxist invectives against the "self-styled masters of language": "Buy one / another or die; but the cultured élite, our squad / of pronouns with their lingual backs to the wall, / prefer to keep everything in the family" ('Questions for the Time Being', 1969). Denise Riley, meanwhile, in her poem 'A Misremembered Lyric' (1993), parodies The Cascades' 1963 hit 'Rhythm of the Rain' ("Listen to the rhythm of the falling rain / Telling me just what a fool I've been") by cross-breeding with the final lines of 'In Praise of Limestone' ("what I hear is the murmur / of underground streams, what I see is a limestone landscape"): "I listen to the rhythm of unhappy pleasure / what I hear is bossy death telling me which way to / go, what I see is a pool with an eye in it".

The most prolific beneficiary of Auden's expansive and inclusive maner, however, was John Ashbery, who wrote admiringly in his undergraduate thesis:

> [Auden] has absorbed certain common techniques of thought (the cataloguing, the characterizing by denoting an unusual quality) and rhythms (those of the cabaret, the birthday card, the political broadsheet) which are very much part of our life, using them to convey ideas which matter very much to us. If he is not a great poet, a decision which must be made by time, he has brought innumerable people closer to the world in which they live.

This argument for the everyday relevance of poetry may seem surprising from Ashbery, a poet who studiously avoided making the kinds of big public statement that Auden was tempted into. The key to his argument, though, is the idea that Auden's poetry brings readers "closer to the world in which they live" – which might be glossed by Sansom's sharp remark that "it is interested in interactions as much as it describes actions". In Ashbery, as in early Auden, the lyric self is immersed in the daily world of half-meanings and mysteries, as it swims towards us through vague waves of weather, news and cliché, murmuring with mysterious urgency (as Veronica Forrest-Thomson observed, Ashbery continued Auden's "variable 'free verse' line which both distances the reader and involves him in its swaying sound"):

Later, the adjustment will be made.
Your boyfriend sips bark tea.

The number should've turned up by now.
Perhaps the driving rain impedes it,
     the recession. In any case there are two too many of us here.
We must double up, or die.

('Strange Things Happen at Night')

Ashbery's apparently facetious rewriting of Auden's line about love, shortly after mentioning "your boyfriend", hints – in John Shoptaw's coinage – at the 'homotextual' tenor of his work, in which the coded world of gay relationships is expressed through a continuous tone of implication (to a homophobic headcount, two boyfriends is "two too many"). As Ian Sansom points out, Auden also allows the shadow of his sexuality to be seen in the opening shot of 'September 1, 1939': the dive on "Fifty-Second Street" was The Dizzy Club, a gay pick-up joint that rejoiced in the Ashberian motto "a rolling tomato gathers no mayonnaise". A silly place, that is, to be serious.

I'm not sure, in the end, whether Sansom's highly enjoyable and illuminating 'biography' makes me like the poem more or less. It certainly makes me wish more literary criticism was written in such a generous and candid spirit (Auden, again, was exemplary in this respect). It also reminds me of why I like Auden's poetry so much, and don't want him to be reduced to his most sonorously general mottoes. *The English Auden* (1977), a gathering of all his writings up to 1939, edited by Edward Mendelson, remains an inexhaustibly original volume. This is the modernist Auden who urged his readers to "Harrow the house of the dead; look shining at / New styles of architecture, a change of heart"; who saw the "lingering [...] white excreta" of a steam train and "first spring flowers arriving smashed"; who magpied the last line of the enigmatic Old English lyric 'Wulf and Eadwacer' for an unrhymed sonnet about a doomed spy ("they would shoot of course, / Parting easily two who were never joined"); and who in a draft of his 'Night Mail' poem, written as the voiceover for a General Post Office documentary, jotted down but didn't use the spectacular simile "uplands heaped like slaughtered horses".

The early Auden was an experimental poet in an unusually independent sense. Reading *The Waste Land* as a student in 1926 was a formative moment, but he did not simply respond with fragmentary laments about dust and typists. Instead, his first long work – published by T.S. Eliot – was *Paid on Both Sides* (1927), a poetic melodrama about an obscure blood feud in the North of England, composed in ominous telegramese ("Reach villages to ask for a bed in / Rock shutting out the sky, the old life done"). Then, in 1932, came *The Orators*, a surreal, noir-ish vision in verse and prose of an economically and politically depressed landscape, written in 1931 as the pound and the second Labour government were collapsing. In this 'English Study', as it was subtitled, failure infects every part of national life (including death: "The priest's mouth opens in the green graveyard, but the wind is against it").

The later Auden held *The Orators* at arm's length, seeing it in 1966 as an incipiently fascist text written by someone "talented but near the border of sanity", whose "schoolboy atmosphere and diction" expressed "rather ugly emotions and ideas". But we don't have to listen to him. *The English Auden* is a more profound book in its appetite for risky truth than the self-consciously moralising verse that followed. When I think of a poet now whose experiments with lyric form have a similarly intense perceptive weirdness and empathetic instinct for the wrong thought in the right words, what I hear are Holly Pester's 'Poems for Idle Workers'. These subversively tender short texts, broadcast on Radio 4 this summer, took the pastoral form of the eclogue to give voice to co-workers longing for human connection on company time. I have no idea whether Pester cares for Auden at all, but I'm pretty sure the author of the queer, quizzical prose poetry of *The Orators*' 'Letter to a Wound' –

> Thanks to you, I have come to see a profound significance in relations I never dreamt of considering before, an old lady's affection for a small boy [...] the partners in the hardware shop on the front

– would admire these fuzzy sentences, spoken sotto voce between sleepy employees Terry and Magatha:

> *Terry*: Can I tune my mood to your coat hook? Our jackets look like resting eagles. What's your day like? Answer slowly, kindly, your voice is a shady morning woodland.

Magatha: Terry, signing-into a logsheet of my heart. Late but not late. You are uncontracted, yet stretched long in the hours we keep. Me? I have a small ache where my clothes fasten. But I'm alright. It cures me to see you.

There are, as Auden once knew, more interesting ways of saying "we must love one another or die" than simply coming straight out with it.

NATALIE LINH BOLDERSTON

Fragments of my mother's homeland underwater
Southern Vietnam will be submerged by 2050
– Saigoneer, Oct 2019

Every place has a name for this.
Here, it is tận thế.

A fortune once told me that *rain is worth everything*
and so I knew that it held all we had ever burned –
pork skewers, begging letters, hell money,
my great-grandmother's remains,
her son's prepared flesh.

In monsoon season, they fused with everything we exhaled.

·

Once, Vietnamese people were said to be descended from Âu Cơ, a fairy
from the mountains, and Lạc Long Quân, a dragon from the sea.

When their forms touched sand, one hundred children climbed out
from black eggs.

·

When the land disappeared,
we poured our ancestors' ashes into Aquafina bottles,
let them live in the ghost of our thirst.

·

Once, we planted peach trees for Tết,
planned to chop and sour the fruit in jars.

Once, the sun slipped so low
that every peach burst on our palms.

We stayed out until our hair singed,
watched black strands split into dust on the concrete.

•

Once, Âu Cơ and Quân spent too long away from home.

Quân tried to hold his human shape, but could not stop his tail from
    growing back.

Âu Cơ tried to cut off her wings and bled a typhoon.

•

Once, a river curdled
at the memory of splitting,

the toxins it was fed
still in the bodies of five generations.

In the bombed cities, waves pull apart reconstructions
of every holy building.

My mother does not cry
because she has already lived through this,

because home is swept away
every minute you're not there.

I hear her voice bend open to red gas,
recede into her mother's toothless murmurs
like names heard through snow.

When we are afraid, it no longer matters that we never learned
to fully understand each other.

•

These days, we are meatless.
My mother still dreams of a pig

fat enough to feed us all for a month,
though we have long since lost our talent for slaughter.

•

Once, Quân threatened a flood so that the sea and land might be joined.

Âu Cơ fled with half her children, taught them to plant khoai lang in pockets
    of warm earth.

Quân carried away all who remained on his back, and they lived as fishermen.

•

Once, there was nothing to hold onto
but the prayers that streaked from my mother's mouth,

her belief that I would live longer if oiled and blessed,
that when she died, there would be someone left

to ask after her bones.

•

Once, we wanted to believe that we'd survive the flood
because we were born from a collision of mountain and sea.

Because nothing has ever held us
as closely as water.

PAULA BOHINCE

Tortoiseshell Comb

Tawny and brown, owlish, heavy as
molasses and honey,
an animal all mouth, teeth bared to bite
the chignon (blond on top

and brunette at the nape)
of this café's one breath-taker,
'coltish', as some girls are called:
long-maned, long-legged.

Silver star at her crown, I trim
Mother's little bangs, kneel on stone
and straighten her head,
slow-walk the scissors.

Outside her house, colts caper
in dusk. A breathless butterfly beats
itself to death, fast then slow,
woozy in leopard air.

With an accident settlement,
her mother bought a mink and some
diamonds, smoked and wore
them under an afghan.

She lifted her visiting children
by the scruff. Mother-tabby: sharp-
clawed, bent. Harrowing against
such gentleness.

Warm, the comb, I imagine.
Sun-suffused as the coin of solitude,
tossed end over end: end-
lessly *beauty*, *horror*, then *beauty* again.

PADRAIG REGAN

Minty

For as long as it takes a single drop of condensation to roll its path
down the curve of a mojito glass before it's lost in the bare wood of the table, everything is held

in its hall of mirrors. Our faces, yes, blown up & stretched grotesquely like balloons,
or inverted in a green liqueur like a cartoonist's idea of alien life. But also:

whatever grid of bricks & wood makes up the room we happen to be sitting in
is dilated & wrapped around a single focal point; whatever portion of the sky that happens

to be visible through the window becomes a convex bowl. The weather also happens,
as it always does, & passes on, & brings those other places where it falls into the orbit of the glass.

It reads the room. It takes things in & what it takes it rearranges on its surface
(or in its core (if they are not the same)) & gives it back for us to read.

So, fish-eyed, myopic, cataracted with dew, a map of a city's erogenous zones
(a patch of grass, a tree that doubled as a lacy umbrella when our shirts were already

soaked transparent, a room full of steam, a jacuzzi's silky jets) establishes a faint legibility, just,
in this green bulb. A mojito or a mint julep? I suspect it doesn't matter much.

Salted Drops
after Ori Gersht

Rembrandt looking like he did
when painted by Rembrandt,
his velveted elbow perched on
a table and thrust towards us.
His gaze is as you would
expect: confrontational & sly.

A hole opens in his face; its
gravity pulls his nose & eye
into itself. & it expands until
his clothes, his ridiculous hat,
are worn by nothing but a
blurry   patch.   Eventually,

the ripples pass & he regains
himself, now framed in an
outwards-moving border of
distorted ovals. The bits of him
first lost – that nose, that eye
– are the first to reappear.

It is a temporary calm; as the
smaller waves rebound, he
vanishes again, but this time
leaves a flesh-pink print like a
cheek rising to the wrong side
of the ice. He focuses,

& now the surface tension is
under less immediate threat, he
flickers through grotesques –
his features re & rearranged –
as the water tries its level best
to   settle   &   tries   again.

ALAN GILLIS

Blossom Drift
22 May 2017

Out the window four or five girls,
six, seven or eight years old,
circle and chitter in some form
of dance or ritual in the garden.

Inside the kitchen table is draped
with bright hoodies, a rainbow
of pencils, bobbles, bangles,
crumbs, puddles of orange juice.

They are constantly on the cusp
of cartwheels, giggles, a wee strut.
Imagine fourteen thousand
of them squeezed into one hall.

If there is a holy war, let heaven
assemble a nation army of pink
deely bobbers and purple nail glitter,
butterfly face paint, marching to a play-

list of Beyoncé, Rihanna, Ariana:
let each follow the steps, learn the moves
of the dance with a gleam in her face
and unclenched fists, free from fear.

See them greet the orphaned daughters
of landmines, drones: each asking
the other "What's your favourite colour?"
and drawing simple pictures of home.

Hear them sing "We found love" together
"in a hopeless place", blossom swirling,
through a dusk that falls from Paradise to here,
over the steeples, domes of Manchester.

The Response

On a day like today you might lift
your eyes to heaven, but better
to lower them, contemplate the yarrow,
the dog daisy, the angel flower,
woundwort, mother of thousands, wild pepper,
goose tongue, snake's grass – better to narrow
your focus upon the thousand-leaved clover.

In the wink of an eye all you know drifts
away but who benefits from sorrow?
The earth still compels you weave a lover's
light flow, although older, sadder:
"I will pick the smooth yarrow
that my lips may be warmer,
that my voice may be gladder."

KIM MOORE

All the Men I Never Married

No. 32

On the way from A wing to B wing
two prisoners start to circle each other

on the long corridor they call the high street,
where the leaves gather in corners

and the wind whistles past the canteen,
past the cell doors, through the high grilled windows.

They push their foreheads against each other,
arms thrown back, their chests pushed out.

A guard shoves me through a gate, a hand
in the small of my back, and locks it.

We watch men emerge from behind closed doors
and gather around the two still locked together.

It's like an old black and white silent movie
except even the black is a washed-out grey –

their jumpers and jogging bottoms,
the doors a darker shade, the walls

an almost white, and just those leaves,
bright spots of colour, stirring a little

before they settle in the corner, brittle enough
to turn to dust if I could touch them

and not a sound from the men watching
or the two who are swinging at each other.

The alarm shrieks and prisoners drop to the ground
like fallen trees and we turn away.

.

At the prison library our men arrive
with poems on scraps of paper in their pockets.

Today Matt is leaving and Jack reads a poem,
asks him to never come back, forget they exist,

and Joe smiles like he's forgotten how,
and Luke tells me it rains in his mind, all the time,

and Arjun tells us about a country
where battles were fought with poems instead of swords

they are listening, some with their eyes closed,
their heads cradled in their arms,

some with their eyes wide open
and when the bell calls them back to cells

they walk out of the room and are transformed,
back to fallen trees, or they become the wall

and never leave, or they transform into a scrawl
of barbed wire and nobody ever touches them again,

or they become the bars of a locked gate
and cast their shadows on each other,

they become the silence, they become the corridor
and men walk up and down inside.

JERZY JARNIEWICZ
translated by Piotr Florczyk

'86

A hefty obscenity in a biography already indecent: I've been alive
longer than my mother. I used to trek to Retkinia to get morphine for her,
to the district's only pharmacy selling it legally.
Doctors from Copernicus Hospital were prescribing minimal doses so that
"she wouldn't get addicted". She lived two extra months. She passed
unaddicted. Several months after her funeral
I invited Piotrek to Łódź. He told the students
about sardines, while they expected a report from a besieged city
– he was nearing forty, but was younger
than my students fresh out of high school.
When he left, I discovered Chernobyl beyond the eastern border,
a May Day Parade marched down Piotrkowska, I fed the kids Lugol's iodine.
Twenty years later I wrote this poem.
If I'm reading it to you, my afterlife continues.
If you're reading it yourself, nothing certain can be said.

Evening Will be Warm, with Returns Possible

Eternal life? Nah, I can't fall for it, but that
the People's Republic would last forever, in that, indeed, I believed
and buried those closest to me feeling the icy breath of that kind of eternity
on my back. The time was right, so we ate chicken noodle soup.
I cleared the table and wiped it clean before
putting all the plates with peace in the dishwasher. There'll be
coffee in the near future, untainted
and within these very walls. In the meantime, you sneak up on me
from behind, as if to make love, so
I don't turn around. From a distance, the dishwasher rattles
like an open heart. I feel you breathing. The final news
from the book of sand, when it's still light out and
the roads are passable.

JAYA SAVIGE

Ladybugs

Your sister etches rain into her skin.
She calibrates the weight of every nick
and then experiments with aquatint
to keep her precious hyphens out of sight.

A paperclip can be a javelin.
The scissors beckon her with open arms.
Yet mostly she prefers the safety pin
she keeps beside the ironed uniforms.

She coaxes ladybugs into the light
from some dark garden thriving in her vein,
as though she were cajoling razor clams
the way her aunties taught her at Yeppoon.

They hatch like fire opals from a vault.
They drip like crimson sequins from a gown.
You know there is a language in the welt
that lifts a pinkish lip to greet each cut,

though nobody can read the cuneiform
she chisels in the tablet of her pelt.
The primitive calligraphy won't scan –
but if you had to parse the hailstorm

you'd say it was her prep for an exam
on how to use her skin to hoard the rain
and navigate a blazing hinterland
without a map, a mother, or a phone.

Tristan's Ascension
i.m. Blaise

The supersonic winds of Neptune might
thrum like this: one billion miles of naught

then whang: the skipping rope at warp speed
in your chest. The custom drumkit of a millipede.

> .

Drummer boy, we know nothing of equilibrium.
But if you catch that air bubble from
the gulp of the waiting room's watercooler,

you will rise like the drowned in Bill Viola,
up through the roof of the sonogram,
and join us in the sunroom.

> .

Oh son. You stepped off one stop too soon.
Your mother has flown

all the way to Titan
to look for you. She bellows to a mound

of electric sand
for a sound, one sound –

or a way to rewind
waterfalls, and rain.

Yes. We will pick you up again, again.

PHOEBE STUCKES

Gold Hoop Earrings

Someone did this to me, I loved him
but that doesn't matter. Having an affair

is just getting all dressed up to cut yourself.
My brain used to shut itself off and go quiet

and fuzzy, the moment he put his hands
on me or took them off. I've tried to imagine

how he felt but I was too busy falling down
my own set of drains. I'm going to spend my life

correcting his attraction to me. I'm different now.
I'll never wear lingerie again. I'm going to acquire

some gold hoop earrings and find someone
to film me talking and talking. I am going

to leave the country, and become
an impressive nightmare, just watch me.

Thus I became a heart-eater

I was holding myself like an open flame
at Candlemas, when the doughnut
presented itself: glossy red and obscene.

The same vague heart-shape
of a woman's face. I ate it
in three bites, in the street, thinking

of Valentine's Day, how every year
it manages to hurt my feelings. How
when I was young I wanted to be called

Valentine, the bringer of love. How
I used to want a minute black heart tattooed
on my buttock, where only a lover could find it,

and what would be the point of that, now?
Then I swallowed and sucked the sugar
from my fingers, like a disgusting child at a fair.

JOHN McAULIFFE

The Robin

The end

of a day, brightening.
Two hours of light.
Locked out, and standing under
where the roof pitches;

a corner of the town
gets in the trees when the west wind
takes it in its July head
to blow and gust.

The blackbird
rushes in and out to the bed and a robin
flickers on and off the lawn, landing
closer and closer to the window, bold,

its beak open and seeming to utter, *you*,
with the hands, one day soon,
this house, everything in it,
a sideways nod, will be gone, or mine.

Steady. It's like
hearing yourself not-think:
green static, red brick.
The key

is at the garage, inside
the *Golf* –
one bad corner and two doors –
where Steve

will have gone into detail
about his wife
leaving him
and the built-in obsolescence

of every motor on the market.
Europe comes into that
too; it does, into
everything. Red brick,

green static. The trees,
falling apart in the late summer.
The door won't open,
I'm outside,

I call to say,
a crackling closeness descending
on the pushed door:
noticing movement,

puffed up, forgetting shadows,
this robin, silent and moving,
tussles with something
on the lawn,

something small,
for practice.

Circumstance

Accession 8, Box 2

The least of the damage from the bombed office
is an elastic band in two parts
on top of a sheaf of translations, "three fifths
from the dead, two fifths
from living languages", notes a handwritten gloss.

There is ash and a smudged print
on the sheet when I move it a little,
a dry scent in the air
as I put everything back in the folder,
including the two pieces of elastic
which still hold all this paper together.

for Michael Schmidt on 50 years of Carcanet

JAY G. YING

Hostel

I fled to my skeleton bunk without warning

I sank into its foam and as I looked around I witnessed signs of the dorm's
other occupants littered on their sheets like loosened haloes

As if I were being crowded out by invisible ghosts
I heard the buzz of bass still playing from one headphone bud left above
and I found it unnerving to witness all those trinkets of sleep

> a map
> a silk scarf
> a ticket stub

> designer cases bursting like imported organs over
> the linoleum so near to me
> > layers of red fabric scattered like soft ore
> > travelling ceremonials out of reach on their beds

I had disturbed the room with my mortal presence
the navy sheet of the stained bedding over my knees like a borrowed skin

I knew I was soon to be walked upon
> to be unmasked as an invader

MEREDI ORTEGA

Biometrics

I pin my right fingers with my left, as if attempting
to flee myself. They're not scanning, the woman
in the post office says. Try warming them.

I rub my hands as though to throw a spark.
As though this booth is an expedition.
Ridges and valleys too dry, contours indefinable.

She tells me to lubricate, watches from her window.
I try again to be British. Over and over, press my
whorls against the screen, which is luminous

green like a pleasant postcard of grass.
Each blade unique, the same. I wipe the glass clean,
reanoint myself, endeavour to materialise.

Another way, according to the BBC: one can slip
one's hand into the epidermis of another
and fingerprint the long-drowned.

Life in the UK

There was a question about bus drivers from
the West Indies. Answer correctly, perhaps we (my
daughter, I) can stay.
Until a great memory lapse. Perhaps a question will
be devised about us, asked of others who come after.
     We, too, have questions.

Why is a radiator? How do we make purchase on ice?
Do we goat hoof/scuttle crabwise on these
dollhouse stairs? What is a second-class stamp?

When I came here, he showed me
reservoir after reservoir, the Derwent Dam was
overspilling, frothing white like a royal wedding train

strung between two towers.
Dear United Kingdom, I fell in love with your water.
     My ancestral rain and green.

The test is only part of the test.
We must run through the forest, hit each tree until
we touch a pot of gold (ding-ding-ding, a rainbow)

payable to the Home Office.
We may/may not advance to the next level.
     Of the following statements, which is correct?
☐ A It resides within, circulates like government
     forms and sludge in pipes.
☐ B We ourselves have forgotten. What is it?

ANJA KONIG

Vogelfrei

Ginger: We'll either die free chickens or we die trying!
Babs: Are those the only choices?
                        – Chicken Run

Once you've flown the coop,
why stop, give up the open road,
return to ground?

Once you've taken orders
only from yourself,
why settle down?

Once you've seceded
why keep the Queen?
Go all the way!

Once you've succeeded,
drilled your own oil,
minted new coin, why not

dissolve your lonely country,
disperse the tribe,
dismiss your outer islands,

count your only vote,
elect yourself and sail
a single acorn into space!

THE GODS AMONGST US

Selima Hill, I May Be Stupid But I'm Not That Stupid, *Bloodaxe*,
£12, *ISBN 9781780371917*
Mona Arshi, Dear Big Gods, *Liverpool University Press*, £9.99,
ISBN 9781786942159
Richard Osmond, Rock, Paper, Scissors, *Picador*, £10.99,
ISBN 9781509894581

Martina Evans considers some searching sequences

. . .

Six poem sequences, each voice telling a different yet interlocking
story, form the body of Selima Hill's *I May be Stupid But I'm Not
That Stupid*. The title is a typically disarming use of litotes because Hill's
narrators are always far from stupid. When she is at her most whimsical
and throwaway, she nails a universal feeling with arresting force:

> Being me is fun. To other people
> the me that I *parade around* in front of them
>
> tossing my big head like a caber
> that wants to be a wedding cake, is not.
>   ('The Wedding Cake')

Hill's narrators may have difficulty connecting in the world but on the page they connect like lightning. The majority of the poems are in couplets, usually in pairs which adds to their crystalline surefootedness. Blakean, they act like subversive bible verses while the long lists of titles, 'My Mother's Ankle', 'My Mother's Sponge', 'My Mother's Purse' form litanies. God might be mentioned on the first page yet his many incarnations as dubious doctors, controlling brothers or the "creepy old man" from 'Lamb Chop' never trump the force of the mother's visceral reality:

> My mother's giant salmon-pink underwear
> is pressed against the bars of my cot
> exuding, in the light of passing cars,
> my mother's sickly smell of warm rubber.
>
> ('My Mother's Underwear')

Cows – denigrated symbols of motherhood – are the most endearing of Hill's signature animals. Refigured and transfigured throughout her collections – here they are made of roses or rubies – they never become tired perhaps because the urgency never goes away: we need to really see them in the same way as we need to see her oddball narrators who are so clear-sighted even if they might toss a "big head like a caber" or "swing the sweetcorn by its hair". The short poems stand alone like proverbs but collectively form a witty continuous dream, a world to get lost in. The virgin, the fallible mother, the female body objectified may be dark subjects, but typically the final sequence where each body part speaks for itself is called 'Helpless with Laughter' – another litany, a wild rosary mocking the Christian fear of the flesh which continues to inform our secular world. The collection began in darkness with the burnt child "lying in my bed in my bandages", a recurring image from Hill's oeuvre, yet despite terrifying perceptions, Hill's rebellious wit always wins, ending in light, however rueful:

> They may well be convenient for slashing
> but wrists are here to keep your bracelets warm
>
> and stop your hands from falling off and anyway
> slashing them doesn't even work.
>
> ('Wrists')

There is more than one god in Mona Arshi's second collection, multiple intriguing voices in fact, reminiscent of Louise Gluck's *The Wild Iris*. 'Little Prayer' opens the book speaking with a tiny precise voice:

> It's me
>   again.
> This time I'm a wren.
>
> Last time I
>   was the first
> white sap.

The voices are ambiguous, creating a tension between the speaker and the poet so we are not always sure who is speaking. As 'Everywhere' opens, it could be the flowers that say, "Mostly we are waiting for the rain." Yet it is the poet who doesn't need to "look in the black / sunflower seeds we take out for / the finches". And he who is "everywhere" is not God, although he could be:

> Yesterday, I saw his eyes
>   in the eyes of a young man next
> to the water-fountain.
>   We tell the children, we should not
>   look for him. He is everywhere.

"He" is the poet's brother, the principle subject here. This is a book of descent reflected in the many indented lines which work like steps as Arshi takes us down into an earth filled with the roots of flowers and plants: "The lilies were sick. / I was new and wifely, / a first tiny garden and / my favourite flower right / by the back door" ('The Lilies'). Juxtaposing lilies, normally associated with death, with the "new and wifely" summons the horrific as they are effectively anthropomorphised, "In the dark with the kitchen lit / they must have peered in, / their occultish hurting faces / pressed against the glass. / They were hard to love back, / these flowers." Later Arshi's flowers speak too, their fractured disturbing voices heard in 'Let the Parts of the Flower Speak':

sepal

My little bastard verses
tiny polyglot faces
how light you are
how virtually weightless.

This is a fine ars poetica: it is when Arshi is at her most delicate, serving her lightest touch that the poems go deepest. Arshi's first collection, *Small Hands*, displayed an array of formal experimentation and she continues to mine that field with prose poems, a cleave poem, a sestina and a tanka along with poetic responses to Lorca, *The Odyssey* and *The Mahabharata*. 'Five Year Update' features very long lines running lengthways along the page, reminiscent of rain or tears, an overflowing of grief barely contained. Yet near the end, it is a much shorter poem with a very long title, 'When Your Brother Steps into your Piccadilly, West Bound Rail Carriage' that leaps off the page, expressing all that complexity so simply, instantaneously:

You could give up your seat, lean forward to touch the hem of
his denim shirt, pull gently on his head-phone wires, say
I am sorry, I'm so sorry.

When the "Almighty" appears on the first page of Richard Osmond's collaged response to the 2017 London Bridge terrorist attacks, I'm tempted to believe that God really is everywhere. Direct poems on Osmond's experience of the attacks are plaited with his original translations from *The Qur'an* and *Beowulf*'s attack on the beer hall. *Beowulf* sits neatly here reminding us of its own tripartite elements where the three agons of the hero's life are interwoven with three different race's histories in order to examine their destiny. And fate and chance are, of course, central to Osmond's strong title poem:

Eight hours into Rob's Stag, which had
started strong with a pub crawl up
the Bermondsey beer mile
and was now beginning to sag

[...]

1. We could go to Katzenjammers
authentic German bierkeller
under London Bridge, where we would
listen to an oompah band, eat sauerkraut
drink litre steins of Paulaner Dunkel
and be held in the basement
by police for our own protection
as terrorists attacked the doors outside

('Rock, Paper, Scissors')

The flat understatement of Osmond's perspective is pitted effectively against the rich cinematics of Beowulf:

under cover of fog
carrying the full weight of the wrath of God
on his shoulders. Grendel:

a reaper with a mind to grab a handful
of mankind.
          Through mist,
he saw the beer hall lit in bright gold

('Grendel came creeping out,')

While the magpie element of this collage reflects Osmond's foraging day job, his knowledge of the countryside has a deeper beneficiary effect as he brings in some lovely working words like "macerated" or "holloway", a word for the "ancient English roads [...] worn into the earth by thousands of years of traffic" and linked to "desire paths in human spaces". Osmond's flair with *Beowulf* made me reach for my own copy again, but *The Qu'ran* sits more uneasily despite or maybe because of a very long note justifying the use of its "heat and controversy". It's a shame that Osmond and his publishers felt the need to contrast a "stereotype of *The Qu'ran* as a monolithic prescriptive text" against the true nature of its real and riddling beauty. Surely this is not a new discovery? The anxiety is, of course, understandable. Placing *The Qu'ran* in such a context is a risk. Perhaps the work would have benefited from more time to mulch down, allowing Osmond the confidence to let it stand on its own. It is when he lets go and moves out of the reader's light that his words hit home hardest:

Only one app loads and works;
it sends me a notification:

*At sixteen weeks your baby is now
the size of an avocado.*

('There's still no signal –')

Martina Evans' latest collection Now We Can Talk Openly About Men *is published by Carcanet.*

REEL VARIATIONS

Paul Muldoon, Frolic and Detour, *Faber, £14.99,*
ISBN 9780571354498

Luke Kennard tunes in to tangential patterns

. . .

In the title poem which closes the book, Muldoon pauses self-consciously to reflect that "it's rare / for me to deviate / from the task in hand". This comes in the middle of a meditation on the wren's reported premeditated tactic of weaving lice-eating spider eggs into its nest, Robert Lowell, The Troggs' discography, the co-opting of indigenous culture by advertising, the Black & Decker sanding belt for which he's trying to buy a replacement and at least a dozen other related tangents, linked as intricately as a complex equation, instinctively as an anxiety dream. "The fact that I've always run two tape reels slightly out of phase / will only partly explain my engagement with the non sequitur / and the leap of the imagination." Readers curious as to the remainder of the explanation for this engagement could do worse than start here, with *Frolic and Detour*, his thirteenth full collection.

Muldoon's poetry is always an education: elegantly cryptic, formally dazzling and as effortlessly musical as it is scholarly. In the age of search engines this oughtn't to put anyone off: it really takes a moment's effort to read up on even the most obscure references. In 'Encheiresin Naturae', a sequence of fifteen sonnets, the title refers to the way, in alchemy, the spirit joins the soul to the body, as referenced in Goethe's *Faust* (alchemists hoped to somehow recreate this substance) and one of the sequence's epigraphs is a proviso from Monsanto: "When farmers purchase a patented seed variety they sign an agreement that they will not save and replant seeds produced from the seed they buy from us." Reappropriated here, it's a perfect, deeply troubling metaphor, and what marks Muldoon out as a poet is his ability to pay attention to this stuff; most of us don't really know what to do with it. The poem blends agricultural, religious and military history and the last line of the sestet provides the image and end word for the first line of the next poem and ongoing rhyme scheme. The sonnet '10' concludes "the moon being merely the stamp of God's wooden leg" and '11' opens "When a forked hazel rod began to shake a leg", for instance, so that every poem contains the seed of the next. As elsewhere, the insouciance of the collective first person makes the erudition charming, a sort of intellectual deadpan: we did this, we did that, "the posts daubed with the blood of a lamb / to protect us from the Angel of Death". Muldoon is really at the height of his powers here. "Despite the pact / between us, God's advances / were mostly unwelcome."

'1916: The Eoghan Rua Variations' is a permutational series of nine near-sonnets, a war song of the Gaelic Irish soldier who took command of the Ulster Confederate Army after the 1641 Rebellion. The poems resolve into an intoxicating pattern in their final quatrains, where the fates of Caesar and Alexander, Tara and Troy are contemplated before turning to "The English? Their days are numbered too"; "The English themselves will shortly be moving along"; "Have you seen the shape Troy's in? / As for the English, that cup, too, will pass"; "Alexander the Great. Great Caesar. Their assorted corps. / Tara is buried under grass. Even Troy's defences broke. / In the case of the English, much the same lies in store." The increasing desperation – "Surely the English will get what's coming to them?" – of the modulated lines is so melodic, wickedly arch and enjoyable it's been going around in my head for weeks.

Much as Muldoon's hallmark joy in form and formal innovation is in evidence here, the imagery is frequently breathtaking. In 'At Tuam', which recounts the poet's ancestors who died in infancy, the tone is movingly compassionate even when at its most acerbic: "At least he would never be forced to thank / the Lord for mercies large or small." It bevels on a central, haunting analogy: "A teenage nun bows before an unleavened / host held up by a priest like a moon held up by an ash tree", a couplet I underlined three times.

Muldoon visits personal teleology and literary autobiography with the same lyrical flair. 'Robert Lowell at Castletown House' returns to the Petrarchan sonnet sequence to provide a mercilessly accurate portrait of the tortured poet as serial monogamist and/or legitimised philanderer: "As it is, he's managed at once to disable / the burglar alarm and lock / himself in"; "When one's weighing wives one must sometimes set a thumb / on the scale." At least, we might reflect, he's not enjoying it: "His penalty so harsh / it was handed down in cuneiform / by Ur-Nammu." I was not familiar with the Sumerian lawmaker known for creating the earliest surviving legal code, but now I am, and my life is richer for it.

There are too many substantial works here to do them justice in a review, but it's nonetheless worth referencing the sheer emotional and thematic range. There are two ekphrastic poems about writers' problematic relationships with alcohol: 'Pablo Picasso: *Bottle of Bass and Glass* (1914)' and 'Georges Braque: *Still Life with Bottle of Bass* (1914)'. The poems are completely identical, listing canonical writers and their habits across seven stanzas: "When T.S. Eliot drank with Valerie Fletcher / she wasn't taking shorthand. / Marianne Moore drank through a snake-scaled hose. / Dylan Thomas drank on his stretcher." It's a scream.

The book is also capacious enough to contain more occasional pieces like 'Belfast Hymn' commissioned by the Grand Central Hotel in Belfast which, in 'How Doth the Little Crocodile' style quatrains, draws comparisons between national diet and national identity. As a passionate fan of complex carbohydrates, I can vouch for the Ulster Fry as "a clear insult to the heart". In contrast to the dough, the long poem is self-consciously light:

> Most of the things we love to share
> are made with cream of tartar
> though any putting on of airs
> is a complete non-starter.

Which would be almost twee if it wasn't so well done and slyly constitutional: "Since we were granted devolved powers / we've all been on a roll."

All of this you can just hook up to my veins forever, but a couple of poems take a more direct approach. 'It Wasn't Meant to Be Like This' is an inevitable lament for the current political situation in the US where Muldoon has lived since 1987. "The news is now not only gobbledygook / but geared, it seems, to what each wants to hear." True enough, but fairly run-of-the-mill for a poet you're accustomed to re-reading five or six times. The poem is strongest in its final lines where there's some questioning of who the "we" actually are: "we did expect to feel self-satisfied, maybe even smug. / It wasn't meant to be at all like this / when we stared into the abyss." This punctures white complacency fairly well even if we've come to expect subtler interventions from a poet who told us absolutely everything about walnuts a few poems back. I'd have been tempted to cut it, along with 'Position Paper' which makes sport of Trump's unique facility for mangling even the most shopworn proverbs. But a monastic needn't evangelise: they draw kindred spirits to them like moths to the light. Muldoon's poetry is already a vigorous rebuke to the worst excesses of the avaricious, the power-hungry and the stupid in its intelligence, nuance and imaginative largesse: it is, and always has been, an act of love and resistance, eo ipso, so I wonder if these more positional poems don't go without saying.

That said, maybe nothing goes without saying now, and our blithe assumption that it ever did is exactly what landed us in this mess. 'Likely to Go Unnoticed', one of the shortest poems in the book, is a triumph. It opens: "Amid acres of rapeseed, a streak of ragwort / may yet shine / as an off-the-record / remark becomes the party line". And it's this rare ability to harness the power of the "two tape reels slightly out of phase" with such purpose, an instinct governed by the wisest heart and mind, not only to notice that which passes most of us by, but to perform a full exegesis, which makes him such an enduringly important poet.

Luke Kennard's latest collection is Cain *(Penned in the Margins, 2017).*

IT'S COMPLICATED

Chen Chen, When I Grow Up I Want to Be a List of Further
Possibilities, *Bloodaxe*, £9.95, ISBN 9781780374864
Stephen Sexton, If All the World and Love Were Young, *Penguin*,
£9.99, ISBN 9780141990026
Theresa Lola, In Search of Equilibrium, *Nine Arches*, £9.99,
ISBN 9781911027683

Alex Pryce on connection and loss in debut collections

. . .

Relationships are, as Facebook has it, "complicated". Nothing is
more complicated than mothers with whom we negotiate the
weight of expectation, loss and independence through all the changing
acts of life. The title poem of Chen Chen's debut collection *When I Grow
Up I Want to Be a List of Further Possibilities* explores the hope to always 'be'
something for others; to be a "good / ex/current friend" or "America for my
uncle, who wants to be China / for me". However, it is the desire "To be
the one / my parents raised me to be" that prevails overall.

Chen's family history appears conventional enough: his family relocated
from China to America as economic migrants seeking a better life when
he was very young. This background pulses through the poems. It is most
explicit in 'First Light', a narrative retelling that opens with the idealised
recollection of the three-year-old who can create an "invented country"

and the white lies of imagined connection, "*Yes it's coming back*". It is his mother's voice that we come to in the end, her view of that "last scent, lost / country". But Chen acknowledges that his mother's voice is "invented, translated (Chinese-to-English, / English-to-English)".

This translation lies at the heart of the collection and it is not merely linguistic but generational and cultural. Chen's America is Harry Potter, *People* magazine and reduced-sodium soy sauce. It is "car[ing] about white people, / especially if they've been kidnapped overseas", but simultaneously feeling that "to further the cause" of Asian-American multiculturalism you should masturbate "exclusively to Koh Masaki, a Japanese gay porn star" ('Talented Human Beings'). For his mother, America is the land of hope for her children's future, "*Doctor, / married to lawyer*" ('Summer Was Forever'), and the growing fear of corruption and loss, "*dirty, diseased, led astray by Western devils*" ('First Light').

The voice throughout is candid but gains troubling energy from teenage sexual shame, doubt and struggle that hangs over and into the humorous self-deprecating voice of the accomplished adult. It is no surprise that both elegies and self-portraits are scattered throughout the book because loss is central to self-knowledge. This seriousness of focus should be hard work, but there is also abundant joy and love in closeness to others and in the experiences that brought Chen to the moments of these poems. This is writing about "salt, noise, struggle, hair, / carrying, kisses, leaving, myth, popcorn, // mothers, bad habits, questions" ('Poem in Noisy Mouthfuls'). In a world of bombastic corporate LGBT Pride and an America publicly grappling with immigrant difference and integration, this is essential reading for "love & forgiveness": "a form of work I'd rather not do alone" ('Poplar Street').

If relationships are work then they are also a form of quest. This is the context for Stephen Sexton's *If All the World and Love Were Young*. While allusion-hunters (or googlers) will note the title of the collection is lifted directly from Sir Walter Raleigh's pastoral love poem 'The Nymph's Reply to the Shepherd', the real frame for these poems is Super Mario World. Yes, the 1990 side-scrolling platform video game from Nintendo.

Like most computer games, Super Mario World is a conventional quest narrative. For the uninitiated, Princess Toadstool (and some dinosaurs) have been imprisoned by the evil Bowser and so the heroes (inexplicably, small plumbers) must make the journey and overcome the obstacles to set them free. Their progress through these 'levels' is charted in the poem titles, all of which come from the game ('Donut Plains 2', 'Chocolate Island 1' en route to the denouement).

This may sound incongruous, but the poems are formally polished and emotionally measured. While they take their titles from game levels, they tackle different temporal and spatial levels. The pastoral of Northern Ireland, the farmer who "continues to plough whose workhorse walks dully along" ('Forest Secret Area'), sits with Classical mythology and the world of the NHS and McDonald's. Sexton is trawling widely for source material to present and understand in a conscious postmodernity:

> Like a labyrinth of neural pathways one encounters dead ends
> and blind alleys and cul de sacs all of which are really the same
> save to say there are various ways of finding yourself lost there
> ('Valley of Bowser 1')

Behind it all the narrative concerns the diagnosis, treatment and decline of Sexton's mother: "cells which split and glitch / so haphazardly" ('Yoshi's Island 2'). It is the private feeling of the semi-public experience of "a radio playing at the nurses' station" and the earth-shattering of "the word for sorry which is the word for we have done / everything within our powers" ('#6 Wendy's Castle'). "What kind of story do I tell", asks Sexton, when Hippocrates comes to say "Today is the day yes I guess" ('#7 Larry's Castle'). The real-life quest does not always have a heroic happy ending.

Memory is the story, even if it is messy and can only be accessed one 'bit' at a time. It is the halcyon recollection of the time before Princess Toadstool went missing, when a child is scrambling aboard a certain "heavy pedalo the likeness of a giant swan" before returning to "our mother on the seafront between the artificial pool / and the sunstruck coastal waters" ('Yoshi's Island 4'). "[W]hen all the world and love was young" there was a television in the corner where a child could become lost in a fictional quest while safe in the family home. Sexton ends with a post-credits scene entreating us to "go out into the world say world it's been so long say world hello" ('Yoshi's House'). The quest is all part of the game.

Theresa Lola's *In Search of Equilibrium* also deals with loss through the technological reference points of the modern world. In this case, it is the decline of a grandfather, a former computer engineer, from Alzheimer's disease. The dissembling of his mental faculties is like a malfunctioning computer: "a memory folder" with "pixelated images", a brain with too low bandwidth until "he realizes he is in the final level of Alzheimer's" ('Alzheimer's Algorithm'). The series of online how-to guides, 'wikiHows', are reimagined as solutions to the challenges the poet faces in 'wikiHow to Find Things You have Lost' and 'wikiHow to Mourn: Mourning in Healthy Ways'. As you might expect, the lived experience is much more complex than the answer provided by a search engine: "Google as the manufactured Garden of Eden" is ultimately imperfect ('<h>Cutting Back on Work Shifts</hr>').

For Lola the struggle of illness in those we are close to also forces a refiguring of Christian faith through the reimagining of biblical texts and forms: "I guess thy will be done in his body, / But on the condition he ends up in heaven" ('The Unedited Version of The Lord's Prayer'). The doubt is expressed well in a retelling of the miracle of Lazarus from the point of view of the mothers whose sons were not resurrected by Jesus: "has his resurrection been an unanswered prayer / because God wants to be the only one bearing / father?" ('Lazarus').

The final poem, a new "last" psalm, presents some hope that God can have mercy for the "typical human / tripping on mistakes" and the anger, dismay, hurt and jealousy of mourning. Lola has found a way through.

Alex Pryce lives in Oxfordshire and writes poetry reviews, features and interviews for various publications.

SUBVERTING PARADIGMS

Legna Rodríguez Iglesias, A little body are many parts, *trans. Abigail Parry and Serafina Vick, Bloodaxe, £12, ISBN 9781780374963*
Darío Jaramillo, Impossible Loves, *trans. Richard Gwyn, Carcanet, £12.99, ISBN 9781784108618*
Mariano Peyrou, The Year of the Crab, *trans. Terence Dooley, Shearsman, £9.95, ISBN 9781848616387*

Leo Boix on Latin American poetry in translation

. . .

W hat are the implications of being a Latin American poet in the twenty-first century? What do the poets consider to be their defining paradigms? Cuban poet Legna Rodríguez Iglesias belongs to the so-called Generación O. This loose group of poets born after 1975 in Cuba has flourished as an alternative cultural scene deliberately setting itself against perceived revolutionary fictions on the island. According to the Brazilian journalist and academic Paulo Antonio Paranaguá, poets of Generación O use sarcasm, deterritorialization, transvestism, fragmentation, colloquialism, hybridisation and adventure "to redesign Cuban identity, recovering their power of subversion".

This is the first comprehensive dual-language edition of the poetry of Rodríguez Iglesias who, as well as eight books of poetry, has written drama, children's books, short stories and a novel. Carefully translated by poet

Abigail Parry and translator Serafina Vick, *A little body are many parts* arose out of a project by the Poetry Translation Centre to bring the three writers together. A principal theme developed by Rodríguez Iglesias is the notion of a collective 'grandfather', a pre-established voice of paternalistic authority that needs to be torn down. Grandfather is an allegorical figure that symbolises Cuba's conservatism, its stifling old traditions and political legacy:

> There are national flowers
> on my *grandfather's* coffin.
> This man fought in a war
> more than sixty years ago.
> A war for freedom.
> Freeing yourself from that which binds you
> is the common struggle.

For the poet, it is a struggle that has radically changed her and her practice, as she embarks on a project to re-write her own history through subversive poetry: "Rest in peace, *grandfather*. / I've been writing, *grandfather*. / And that is *my* revolution" ('Fertile Truce'). The notion of a collective grandfather appears again in 'Spoilt', where the tensions between past and future, of following a tradition and breaking away from it, will ultimately lead to questioning the nationalistic patriarchy itself.

> Bad behaviour:
> saying to grandfather
> *screw the fatherland*
>
> Good behaviour:
> saying to grandfather
> *hooray for the fatherland!*
>
> All the while
> saying to grandfather
> *your country is my country*

A sense of rebelliousness and cynicism permeates most of Rodríguez Iglesias's work, leaving the reader in a state of restlessness. Her poems are full of sharp, staccato-like stanzas, where irony, dark humour, and at times deep sadness, are combined. In 'No flowers for me', written after moving to Miami in 2015, the poet explores the seemingly opposite themes of migration and exile, embodied through a sense of loss and nostalgia for her hometown of Camagüey. However, as with the notion of subversion seen in attitudes to the grandfather figure, poetry, for Rodríguez Iglesias, offers the possibility of rebirth, of starting anew and leaving behind "suffering and pain, that ought to die".

> No flowers, if I die in Miami.
> If I die on the highways of Miami.
> Don't you remember that sweet time,
> my sugar? The love that's behind me
>
> is gone. There are better days
> under the pavement – they flourish
> as I walk along. There's a muscle
> for suffering and pain, that ought to die.

Impossible Loves, by the Colombian writer Darío Jaramillo, is also the first time a selection of his work has been translated into English. This dual-language collection, full of witticisms and lyrical meditations on everyday life, showcases one of the greatest living poets from Latin America. Jaramillo was born in 1947 in Santa Rosa de Osos, a town in Colombia's northern uplands, the location for many of his poems on childhood memories. Translated by the award-winning writer Richard Gwyn, editor of the seminal anthology *The Other Tiger: Recent Poetry from Latin America* (Seren, 2016), this sampling of Jaramillo's work is full of intellectually refined poems. Although in his foreword Gwyn points to Nicanor Parra as a main source of inspiration for Jaramillo, the work of Jorge Luis Borges is also important. In 'Another Ars Poetica I: Time', one of many poems that deals with the complexities of time, the poet describes the qualities a poem should have if it is to stand up as a work of art:

> Of the geometry of time this poem that runs over
> the cold skin of minutes that neither wait nor pester,
> of the line of days sown in the metallic light of the dead,
> forced to flower by such life as flows in their water-clock veins.

Of time this poem peering sideways at death, of time
brother of nothing, of weightless time gravitating
above my head and above the head of my brother, of time
this poem, of time that walks on water and passes through

The preoccupation with past time also marks his 'Nostalgia' sequence, as in 'Nostalgia, 3' where the poet attempts to recover a delicate memory from an idealised childhood in Antioquía:

To dilute memory in a kind of wistful stupor,
unhurried hummingbird who lists the warmest places,
bewildered memory,
cold mirror of another time's heat

Gwyn's selection, from a poet whose career spans five decades, shows Jaramillo at the height of his powers. He is as comfortable writing about the seemingly mundane, from a gum tree, a cat, stones or mangoes, to the art of poetry, the impossibility of love, and musings on Plato. His is a poetry full of paradoxes and intellectual sensibilities that leave the reader enraptured by his revelations:

I have experienced absolute clarity:
the light is perfect to bring out the precise profile of things,
shadow makes up an element of light, helps us to see:
this tree corresponds to the archetype I remember,
everything adjusts to the idea,
this petal is the eternal petal
and tomorrow will be the eternal whitened petal
('Plato, Drunk')

Mariano Peyrou, born in Buenos Aires but resident in Spain since childhood, is also preoccupied with time, describing memories as scuttling sideways like a crab, sometimes disappearing, then re-emerging from the sand. *The Year of the Crab* consists of a narrative poem in three parts that each relate to an endless summer, or possibly various summers fused, spent by the poet and his family at their holiday home in Galicia, Northern Spain: "In the year of the crab we used to walk sideways so as not to wake anybody." Peyrou's crab has pincers that:

appeared in the sand in our glimmering imaginations and we were fearful and cheerful. In the rest of the land slaves to reality spoke of the economy. The children turned nasty.

('The Year of the Crab')

These children inhabited a house of the past that "began to fill with questions". Questions that could easily turn into terror: "We had a crab in our mouth, and you had to be careful with it, chew slowly so it didn't wake."

Translator Terence Dooley succeeds in keeping the original musicality in the English, skillfully recreating the lyricism and lucidity of the poems. The book, according to Dooley, "is a story poem with a musical structure. Its three movements, as in a concerto, contain recurring motifs and themes which, as they return, develop and intensify". There are many characters: from the narrator who is sometimes a child among other children, to Inés, an idealised woman or girl, the telegraphone, a mythical beast, and She, a mother-figure who is ill and cannot take part in the games of the summer. And of course the crab, which appears in many guises. I was struck by how Peyrou's use of simple, almost childlike language could unpick so much fear, love, nostalgia, terror, as well as a growing sense of loss. The complex symbol of the crab, with all its nuances and associations, imbues the collection with symbolic weight, allowing for many enriching readings and interpretations:

Sometimes he picked them up by one leg and held them
up in the air. The crab seemed to be dancing, hanging
in a tiny sky, waving its other nine legs, maybe hopeful, maybe terrified, maybe just going about its business, maybe dreaming of drawings it wouldn't appear
in again for a good while, feeling one leg, nine legs,
while a vast strange universe decided its fate
unhurriedly, unworriedly.

('The Year of the Crab')

Leo Boix is a Latinx-British poet, journalist and educator, born in Argentina.

GATHERING INTENSITY

Vona Groarke, Double Negative, *The Gallery Press*, €11.95,
ISBN 9781911337607
Deryn Rees-Jones, Erato, *Seren*, £9.99, ISBN 9781781725108

Claire Crowther on hope, age and the lyric impulse

. . .

Double Negative, by Vona Groarke, sounds like a book for our times,
given the current political binaries. Seventeen poem titles direct
you specifically to fight the negative: 'Against Anxiety', 'Against Despair',
'Against Boredom' etc. Groarke is a teacher and in a lecture at Trinity
College Dublin once admitted that, while teachers would tell poetry
students to go easy on abstract nouns, she herself was drawn to the idea
of using abstraction to make two words "chafe against each other" and
then "agree in some odd or unforgettable fashion". 'Against Melancholy'
has that odd quality she was looking for:

> There now. Seems I stared it down.
> Let the evening shake itself dry like a dog
> so the tail is the last thing wriggiggling
> as, of course, you knew it would be.

In this book, the very idea of the poem as a piece of writing is somehow negative, as in this ars poetica:

> This is the poem that won't open
> no matter where you press.
>
> This is the poem that cries on street corners
> and plays at being lost.
>
> This is the poem arranged at a tilt
> so all the words slide off.
>
> ('This Poem')

Groake's words do indeed slide off their obvious meanings, and that has always been a delightful feature of her work because the angle of the slide is so finely judged. 'Aftermath Epigrams', the last poem, is a more far-ranging ars poetica:

> From annal to analysis:
> every day is words blindfolded
> and made to walk the plank.
>
> [...]
>
> If it's a poem
> it should have people in it.
> I don't see anyone.
>
> [...]
>
> A day without a volta
> is a day with nowhere to hide.

If that reads like a farewell, there are indeed many farewells in the book – a child leaves home, passers-by pass by, even the ocean will withdraw:

> I wait as the keyhole waits
> for the ocean to get up from its white chair,
> shuck off these silky metaphors
> and, cursing my every idleness,
> take itself off down the shingle path

that, obsequizing every step,
has nothing, all the while, to say to me.

('The Picture Window')

What words offer the attentive poet as she ages, Groarke demonstrates, is
the usual fun with form; there are prose poems here, epigrams, a sonnet.
And she mentions the word 'metaphor' often, possibly because an
overarching metaphor in the collection is the one where words are life and
life is telling her something important:

The rain doesn't care so much for lists.
Tonight it calls by the house late
with something important to say.

Its words end in all double letters
that lean in, like italics,
close to each other
so nothing comes between.

('Against Loneliness')

I find Groarke hopeful: beneath the book's awareness of ageing, beneath
the domestic minutiae that is present in almost every poem, beneath the
despairing pairing word play, there is a drive to avoid the simple binary
of good versus bad. The first stanza of 'A to Z' shows that words might
usefully chafe together but so might facts:

Say one thing and straight away the opposite
hoves into view. That is why, perhaps, I am
indefinite – something to do with being Libran
or being short and therefore always riddled with
comparative fact.

[...]

We are so small. We put tins
in cupboards and we take them out again.
We forget to eat. We eat. We love.
We only wish we could.

Bewildered now? In the mindset of a Groarke poem I always have been, yet I'm always hooked. *Double Negative* is the seventh collection from a poet who may be more abstracted but is gathering, rather than diminishing, in intensity.

As in *Double Negative*, much of the material in *Erato*, Deryn Rees-Jones's fifth collection, now shortlisted for the T.S. Eliot Prize, swings between elegy and ageing.

> What stepping in
> and back and on
> is this, this middle age?
>
>   ('Firebird')

Also like Groarke, Rees-Jones is a teacher as well as a poet. There is a sense, throughout *Erato*, of the poet holding experience up between thumb and forefinger for the reader to examine. 'Mon Amour', for example, the first poem in the book, is a long prose poem, each section ending with an unspoken question: what do you make of that?

> The man who lived in the adjacent house in the terrace stopped me in the street one day and told me I was a disgrace to my profession. I was not even sure he knew what I did. Later he wrote me an unsigned letter, reinforcing my need for personal shame, insisting I cut down the tree in my backyard which towered across the rooftops.

This detachment transmits a sense of numbness that suits the elegiac material, but also registers seismic shocks when Rees-Jones is overwhelmed by lyric feeling. She is a master of elegy as her last two collections have shown. She counterpoints calm and agony, mature reflection and revulsion. 'Mon Amour' ends thus:

> From the edges of my vision I was sure I saw a wolf slip with its yellow eyes from behind the bookcase to the room next door. I didn't want to check. The room was filled with a strange scent. Then the doorbell rang. The screen flickered. Skin. Bones. A doctor had said to me, We will watch, and wait.

Something I knew was only beginning.
Something, I knew, was at an end.

Rees-Jones's poems often hinge in this way, choosing (conventionally) flora or fauna or hard weather to open the lyric latch: "The common laurel which I plan to fell / today can stand for love, this hell" ('I.M.'). But 'Drone' begins with politics, "I am listening to an interview with a man whose job it is to program drones", and becomes a recount of lost sexual love while deftly shaking time loose. Transcending the actual is, of course, a normal poetic aim and in this poem Rees-Jones brilliantly exposes it in a way that forces the reader ("you") and the narrator ("you") to identify with the narrator's lover ("you"):

As I listen, the glass in the window shatters. In slow-motion you are reversed back into the evening, shaking time off your heels.

In a matter of seconds you have disappeared. I think about nectar and pollen and honey and my whole face bursts into flames.

'Fires', equally inclusively, asks:

What happens

if we

figure the lyric though this trauma, this movement in time between the workings of our unconscious/imagination, our connection with the moment of perception, being alive, and real?

'Fires' is an academic's meditation on death and children, specifically the loss to her children of their father, and it breaks up parental anxiety with analytic rigour:

Like the after effects of trauma the fires keep returning, re igniting. I chance upon a late, unfinished poem by Elizabeth Bishop which recalls an incident in her infancy as she watched the nearby town of Salem being consumed by flames. 'A Drunkard' is a poem full of repetitions, verbal doublings –

'clearly clearly' 'reprimand reprimand'

– a particular tic in Bishop's work, which appears to occur at moments when the 'nagging thoughts' that cannot quite be understood poke through.

Erato is the Greek muse of lyric poetry, summoned up in the book's Virgil epigraph to witness the poet's own witnessing of many horrors. Such a literary muse is a good model for an academic disquisition on poetry, its erratic nature, its erasures and errors, as is Barbara Hardy (a literary scholar) honoured in '13 Numbered Fragments Keeping Barbara Hardy in Mind'. This witty nod to Wallace Stevens' 'Thirteen Ways of Looking at a Blackbird' mulls over the "bad reader [...] the fearful reader, the reader in a hurry to be determined". We stand corrected. So do poets; the poem names poetic practice as "'Failure in practice'. 'Getting things wrong'".

In that poem, mis-takes are the creative point. Though this may be a professor in emotional distress while over-controlled by a bookish world, with a tone too bookish sometimes, still her lyric gift flies round the well-stacked library and sings:

Listen to the nightjar, hear her holy tremblings –
star litter, night fragment, slip down a spine of grass.
               ('Nightjar')

Claire Crowther is the author of three collections and co-editor of Long Poem Magazine.

THE WATERWHEEL AND THE CAR WHEEL

The Collected Poems of Bertolt Brecht, *trans. Tom Kuhn and David Constantine, W.W. Norton, £35,* ISBN 9780871407672

Alistair Noon on the poetry and politics of Brecht

. . .

In 1927, the judge of a German poetry competition opted not to award a prize to any of the four hundred poems entered, reporting that all of them were – quite literally – "useless". The judge was Bertolt Brecht, and there were plenty of reasons for a German writer of his time to consider how poetry might or might not be useful, not least the living conditions of the German working and workless poor: when Brecht wrote about the hungry, he was (again) being literal. The usefulness of literary work would become even more of an issue for him later, when the Nazis took power and he went into Scandinavian exile, and then in America where he witnessed how advanced capitalism affects everyday human interaction.

A perceptive recorder of his own exile experience, and an observant political chronologist, Brecht is best known as a poet for his encapsulations of historical moments, frequently framed as rhetorical questions. Tom Kuhn and David Constantine's sweeping new twelve-hundred-page translation includes such classics. "Why do I watch the changing of the wheel / With impatience?" Brecht asks as the realities of the nascent GDR dawn on him in 1953 ('Changing the wheel'). Fourteen years earlier he writes: "What times are these, when / A conversation about trees is almost a crime / Because it entails a silence about so many misdeeds!" ('To those born after'). The fact that a conversation about trees is one of the things worth having right now only brings Brecht's point, made in an era of fascist ascendancy, better home.

Not atypically for famous poets, however, Brecht's most famous poems are atypical. His political poems are more often answers than questions, favouring forms that afford maximal didactic scope: the fable, the hymn parody, the mock nursery rhyme, and above all the ballad, the latter often with lengthy, even unwieldy refrains. Brecht certainly gets closer to a genuinely political poem than most poets do, not merely raising social issues and demands but articulating an actual agenda: whether, in repurposing poetry for the social struggle, he articulates a new subjectivity is more moot.

His early work thinks hard about why people at the hard end of the economic system fail to act to improve their own lot. He has an eye for the daily dilemmas faced by those living at or below the subsistence minimum, and sees that the poor bear the brunt of wars that are not in their interest. He identifies the delusions of capitalism and fascism but falls, perhaps knowingly, for the illusions of Stalinism and its by no means innocent precursor, Leninism. As he begins to see Russian-led state socialism as the only viable vehicle for resistance and change, poems start to dabble in the relevant personality cults. But a criticism of such cults can be read in 'Empedocles' shoe', a version of the tale of the Greek philosopher's death: Brecht has him lay a false trail to delay his disciples' discovery of his leap into Etna. Fascinatingly, the final pages of this volume include Brecht's versions of full-on anti-Stalinist poems by the Polish poet Adam Ważyk.

Brecht is good on the Nazis, revealing their warping of language, the impossibility of their promises, and the instrumental nature of anti-Semitism, as well as mercilessly dissecting the complicity of Germany's industrial, judicial, medical and media elites in the regime. Yet a poem such as 'The Song of the SA Man' is a 'we-wuz-deceived' fantasy that tries to explain away how large parts of the German proletariat had turned sharp right, contrary to what they should have done according to Marxist theory, a fantasy in fact denying them the agency that the theory accords them. This exculpatory view ironically aligns Brecht – on this point – with the immediate post-war West German consensus (and got him into a spat with his fellow literary exile in Los Angeles, Thomas Mann, who thought post-war Germany deserved everything coming to it).

The contradictions continue. Brecht has a sensibility for issues specifically weighing on women in the world he describes, including childcare, exploitative relationships and prostitution. There are eulogies and elegies for the women in Brecht's life who did the legwork to facilitate his writing, including Helene Weigel, Margarete Steffin and Ruth Berlau. But while seldom belittling women directly, he nevertheless objectifies, ventriloquises and subordinates them, leaving a sense of misogyny that pervades the early work and peppers the later. Most fundamentally, Brecht instructs his readers to think for themselves, while largely excising ambivalence and ambiguity from his poems. With his exhortations to do this and do that, Brecht situates truth within (his) text and not in its relationship with the reader, in the generalisation rather than the specifics.

The translator-editors help make sense of this sprawling, conflicted work with pertinent introductions and judicious notes (in the case of an otherwise dreadful poem called 'Sauna and sex', they include the amusing information that Brecht signed it in his notebook as "Thomas Mann"). They give us many poems I doubt the later Brecht would have considered useful, revealing the subcurrents and latent alternative paths in his work: his very early quasi-Expressionism, not yet inflected by irony and self-righteousness, and lyrical, personal poems, all passed over in *Hundert Gedichte*, the last major gathering of his work in his lifetime, presumably for lacking usefulness.

There's a lot to get in Brecht: the oscillation between low and high marked forms in the obscene song and mock German classical hexameters, between the carefully versified and the prosaic. Over such a long stretch, form is inevitably reflected with varying degrees of intensity in the translations, but 'Song against war' is one of many bullseye renditions with the meaningful rhymes it finds in English ("victorious" / "wars for us", "classes" / "masters"). Another is 'The ballad of the waterwheel':

And the waterwheel just goes on turning
Fortunes come and go – you know the deal.
While the water down below must keep on churning
Its only business is to drive the wheel.

A further issue is what to do with the brutality of much of Brecht's language, which catches – but also re-sounds – the militarised tone that prevailed in German between the rise of the Prussian officer class in the late nineteenth century and 1968. In 'A ballad for Article 218', a male doctor bullies a woman out of an abortion in a pull-yourself-together and do-your-national-duty way. In the translation, the doctor is paternalistic but also a little avuncular. Notwithstanding the poet's, translator's and reviewer's lack of first-hand experience of this situation, this could be a plausible cross-cultural or cross-temporal translation, cashing in historical specificity for immediacy. Across the translations, the brutality seems somewhat toned down in the English, likely for want of an immediately available counterpart in the more genteel, obfuscatory language of the British Empire.

Much of Brecht's work is not a polite reaffirmation of beauty and wonderment for those with the time to wonder, but a gauntlet thrown down before liberal democracy, certainly in its guise prior to the welfare state. Can you feed us? Can you clothe us? Can you save us from fascism? But despite the efficacy of the Soviet Union's PR machine, and notwithstanding the sheer necessity of opposing the Nazis, there were causes for doubt about the line Brecht took even before he got to live in a Stalinist state himself: the Soviet Union's lethal political scapegoating in the 1920s, the show trials of the 1930s, the Hitler-Stalin pact of 1939. The fact that when exile became imperative for Brecht he chose Scandinavia and ultimately the US rather than the USSR has long been cited as evidence that he had some knowledge of what was happening there (and could have happened to him). Where Brecht does let doubt into his poems, they frequently resolve back to certitude, as if he were a job interviewee admitting to impatience as his greatest weakness, only to demonstrate his drive.

Hannah Arendt, who wrote at length about Brecht, carefully differentiated between philosophy and politics, the former concerned with truth, the latter with power. Where does poetry fall? The first Brecht poem I read, as a student, was 'Beds for the night', in which he cleverly – usefully even – flips round the lines of his preceding stanza to show that charity will never change the world. I remember being very convinced by its argument, and now wonder why Brecht, watching his driver changing the car wheel, doesn't go and get him a coffee.

Alistair Noon's translations of selected poems by Osip Mandelstam, Concert at a Railway Station, *were published by Shearsman in 2018. He lives in Berlin.*

SLIP-SHAPE AND MIND SPACE

Alice Oswald, Nobody, *Cape, £10*, ISBN 9781787331969
Peter Riley, Truth, Justice, and the Companionship of Owls,
Longbarrow Press, £12.99, ISBN 9781906175382

Linda France on song lines of constancy and flux

. . .

Although written under the influence of a long-term exchange with the artist William Tillyer (and originally published in an edition with his watercolours), *Nobody* begins where Alice Oswald's long poem *Dart* left off – in the fluid, open space where a river becomes sea. It is the realm of a watery god identified as:

> all names, all voices, Slip-Shape, this is Proteus,
> whoever that is, the shepherd of the seals,
> driving my many selves from cave to cave...
> (Dart, Faber, 2002)

In this new work, Proteus is joined by other 'nobodies' who inhabit liminal spaces in Classical myth. The long poem dwells on the constant of change, what happens when one thing is juxtaposed with another and, losing its edges, turns into something else, just as one colour of paint bleeds into its neighbour diluted with water and creates a new shade. The sea is both itself and metaphor – a space we can carry (ourselves) across – as we are immersed in its unknowable vastness and experience the profound interplay of particle and wave: "How does it start the sea has endless beginnings". The fertile murkiness between stories, people, things and elements is an atmosphere in which Oswald can seek words where none usually reside, a blank field for her restless curiosity, her imaginative heft and dramatic talent for ventriloquism.

With varying degrees of broken and elided syntax, their recourse to repetition, trailing slippages of time, colour and space, all the different voices are asking: where does one thing begin and another end? Oswald interrogates the idea and experience of perception and creation, testing the limits of language and form, all at sea:

> Why is my mind this untranslatable colour of scratchiness and
>   indecision

Her exploration of the mists between similarity and difference, connection and isolation, love and betrayal, is a mythic quest for the source of things and the stories and songs seeded there: the generative friction between opposites, "light and unlight", "cloud / uncloud". The looking and the asking sets other possibilities in motion, endless choices – "I wish I was there or there" – ultimately finding "no one" or "nothing":

> this disintegrating certainty this water
> whatever it is whatever anything is
> under these veils and veils of vision

A recurring verb is "floating" and these fragments of tales within the whole poem rise to the surface like flotsam. Speaker and listener, subject and object move back and forth. When a "muse" is called upon for further information about "this floating nobody", "this ancient passer-by", there seems to be no answer, only (later) the terse assertion:

> you know full well he said this is only the water
> talking to us in the voice of amnesia

Deserted even by memory, the search for the beginning of things turns into an ending, where the poem's voices become one with the sea and appear as dramatis personae in a continuous expanse of text, settled in the lower half of the final pages. Their names merge and fade, certain individuals picked out in a darker font: "ODYSSEUS... ORPHEUS... CLYTEMNESTRA... AEGISTHUS... CALYPSO... CIRCE... POSEIDON... NOBODY".

Perhaps unsurprisingly, given the collaboration with Tillyer, a "crowd of colours" keeps surfacing, "all the shades of mauve green blue", brown and coppery pink, "seemingly endless yellowness" and purple spreading like a series of bruises. Many sea birds pass over, the precise detail of their forms and names (heron, guillemot, sea raven, osprey, cormorant etc) sharp against the water's edgelessness. Even among the human population, feathers fly as engines of articulation: Icarus's wings here, a "feathered smile" there. The birds and bird-like creatures recall the souls of the dead, ancestors flocking and clamouring to be heard. The poet listens, straining to locate the source of the voices – including her own – while the only constant is the sea, timeless, matrix and destroyer. Astonishing lines and transitions wash up on every page, weathered by the flux of the tides. Oswald's pitch and rhythm is seductive, marvellously dangerous. Like all good stories, this is a voyage of transformation, rooted in the body, when the impossible can happen, "where the cold of swimming is no different from the clear of looking".

Although Peter Riley's *Truth, Justice, and the Companionship of Owls* is "earthfast", its coordinates in the Upper Calder Valley clearly identified, far from Alice Oswald's southern seas, the two collections have unexpected territory and preoccupations in common. Both de-centralised, non-urban, un-metropolitan, they share an interest in convergences, the potential of inbetween spaces, keen "to notate while we can / between anger and tears the last waltz, the song left over" (Riley, 'Ring Cairns'). Both poets are committed to an elegiac transparency, pleasing yet disarming. We are held witness to grief, disappointment, rage and consternation at the state of things, "all our old questions" ('Ring Cairns').

What is seen as lost or absent in Riley's work is not so much "nobody" as "nowhere": the ancestors (and the narrator's voice) speaking through this "hard, wet, cold, nothing land" ('Nine Poems'), where "all the hills and rivers are of course / the vocabulary of our lamentation" ('Hushings'). Four sequences – two of which previously appeared as pamphlets – chart passages through this "true north" of moors, intersected by stone, a network of buses and trains, canals and pubs, the Co-op and Trades Club.

Above ground, there are birds and snow, stars and "mind space". Thomas Hardy is a suitably brooding "guide and spokesman", alongside other companions, living and dead – "a crowd worth joining" to protest against the accumulation of "human harm", the unjust treatment of the disadvantaged and displaced, and the inequitable distribution of wealth, power and privilege.

Almost a character in itself, the economy casts a long shadow over the land and its people: "there are bills to be paid" among "the ruins of commerce" ('Hushings'). The balancing of accounts is necessarily both personal and political, the first-person voice often leaning into the plural: "Tell us it has not been all in vain" ('Pennine Tales'). Address and tone keep shifting, negotiating a vocal register suitable for the changing gradient, a crossing between movement and stillness, solitude and society. Memories of being taught 'All Things Bright and Beautiful' as a child prompt intimations of the inculcation of a "slow and solemn trust [...] wrapped around the heart, the dark simplicity of mutuality" ('Hushings'). Here, as in Oswald's *Nobody*, there are beginnings and endings – in particular, a sense of a review-in-progress after "the rusting of the years" ('Hushings').

Riley, perhaps, grants more room to hope than we might expect: the word is repeated as if being regularly stress-tested. Although sometimes found wanting, it "stands firm in the common tongue", sure of its light, despite constant incursions from the dark:

> And in
> all this land, this nothing-much, there are
> hidden values, seeds waiting to announce themselves
> as cotton grass and bugle.
> ('Hushings')

The engine that keeps hope running is the endurance of working people, offering evidence of survival also to be found in the landscape itself, particularly the limestone "hushings" and "ring cairns" that give their names to two of the sequences. All of the poems, buttressed by their twelve- or three-line forms, communicate a sense of substantiality, resistance. More contemporary circles, nodding at archetypal associations of continuity and unity, are wittily summoned in the turning circles of buses that weave their way up and down the valley, connecting place and population in daily lives "where people do what they usually do" ('Pennine Tales'). This is Time as the ongoing moment as well as an echoing down from prehistory, deftly exposed in the strata of this compelling and persuasive collection.

Classical and other literary and musical allusions are riffed upon in a coda of notes and 'Scribal Glosses (homage to the Master of the Macclesfield Psalter)'– a process which, Riley states, "can continue indefinitely, and at a certain point will be taken out of my hands". Meanwhile, love is there as "a gravitation", and poetry waits to transport us "like an old minibus in a garage while / we sleep, slightly losing oil" ('Hushings').

Linda France's most recent collection is Reading the Flowers *(Arc, 2016).*

AMBIVALENT ZONES

Miriam Gamble, What Planet, *Bloodaxe*, £9.95,
ISBN 9781780374840
Kei Miller, In Nearby Bushes, *Carcanet*, £9.99,
ISBN 9781784108458
Helen Tookey, City of Departures, *Carcanet*, £9.99,
ISBN 9781784107598

W.N. Herbert on real and imagined landscapes

. . .

These three collections concern themselves in contrasting, innovative ways with the tensions between our imaginative apprehension of place and the often-resistant realities of places themselves. In Kei Miller's case, perceptions of Jamaica play out wittily through dialect and toponym, and are set against violent circumstances, explored with a profound awareness of their cultural and historic causes. For Helen Tookey, place becomes a series of intense encounters with the territories of European artists, in which their settings or personalities – and the poet's – mingle or erode.

Miriam Gamble's *What Planet* contrasts themes of home and visitation with an unsettling control of tone and imagery, locating meaning in sudden symbolic gestures of freedom, or perspectival shifts. One such shift occurs in the last line of 'Kitten', where uncertain demarcations of memory ("In what you remember as the dark but / can't have been given it was summer") contrast with a glimpse of the speaker as if seen by the kitten in its carry box: "Your face against the grid, blunt as a shark".

Inanimate objects are granted their own near-autonomy, sometimes putting the characters in these poems in their place. In 'Girl with Book and Rubber Bands', the girl has attached the volume "to a string of rubber bands" and treats it like a yoyo, "sending out and reeling [it] in [...] on a rubber leash", causing traffic to come to a standstill and her witnesses to decide that "we like the cut of her jib more than / anything". Self-reflexiveness creeps in as the girl and her friend achieve a joyous liberation, "Their shoes [...] nowhere to be seen." This could be read as referring to the collection, in which several poems are produced in "collaborative conversation" with another poet, focusing on the 2014 Scottish "IndyRef".

Such elasticity extends to the syntactic flow of these poems, as in the anaphoric incantation of 'In the Annum', which settles itself in a time "before": "In the annum of the water bomb", "of the girl's shoe with / a key in the heel", "In the annum that preceded / *American Beauty*". However, these apparent innocences are set against a sense of impending threat summed up in the first poem's intimate dread of "a provisional touching your father's hair" ('The Landing Window Is Unspeakable'), and embodied in the later elegies for the poet's mother.

The mating dance of the bird of paradise (or parotia) seems to embody Gamble's sense of the un-chancy nature of liberty as something both compulsive and absurd: "Say / that the brown bird looking on gives audience / only in the sense that Commodus gave audience" ('Parotia Displaying in a Forest Clearing'). The echo of "parody" here points equally to parable or satire: no sooner is the bird seen as a "defrocked cleric" than its mate is being directed as though in a strange farce: "Under the light of a supermoon / let the watcher make haste to the village hall".

These elements come together in the sestina 'Betty Staff's', in which a grandmother presides over a dancehall despite impending social changes and the spectre of domestic abuse:

> more than once he will knock her to the floor, and free of breath.
> But to the jewel-clad notion of the post-war 1950s,
> Betty will play the mother octopus – *Lengthen your neck. Die nacht*
>   *ist wunderbar –*

Kei Miller's poetry is constantly locating itself while dislocating the reader's sense of a stable ground from which to consider it. Its setting, Jamaica, is sure enough, but as the cartographer of Miller's previous collection found, Jamaica is itself a place of "immappancy" in which our sense of place is reconsidered and renewed. That critique continues here – "here" being both island and page – in the transitions of what he calls the understory, where epical matters such as arms and the language in which we speak of them shift meanings:

Here that cannot be held

by the small arms of language.
     Here that cannot be held
by the small arms of English.

     Here that cannot be held by the English.
          ('Here Where Blossoms the Night')

The very flora and fauna – those perpetually "nearby" bushes, an escaped herd of reindeer "without snow" ('Here Where Run the Wild Deer') – and an underlying geological instability, all contribute to this perpetual revision of how we believe ourselves to be somewhere, glimpsing through this "the quiet that is not quiet / this peace that is not peace" ('Hush').

In the book's central section, 'Sometimes I Consider the Names of Places', the etymologies of naming and the strategies of recycling names create doubled places and erase existing ones, "as if this world was not enough". This imposition of naming pushes Miller's attention towards the unnamed in 'So What Will We Call the Thing Between Places':

Like hiking up a mountain – that thing between one village and the
   next, between the
long sit downs, the stretch between the stretch? What do you call it
   – that interruption
of miles that might smell of eucalyptus, that limbo of land

Desire, transgressions and imaginative possibilities all cluster in such ambivalent zones which, in the book's titular final section, contain murder. Here, the page and the body of the murdered woman seem to double each other, as newspaper accounts are repeatedly sifted for implicit text, picked out in bold, while an extraordinary posthumous narrative depicts the murder victim:

> Already the worms are rising, pulling towards you, towards the thing
>   you once
> considered you: the body. You had a heart; it stopped. Then things
>   began to happen.
>   ('III')

This "useless energy of ghosts" ('XI.I') is redirected with great tenderness into a vision of the tension between our deep need for security and the violent insecurity of our needs, and how this plays out across gender, history and race. The book ends with the reiteration of a prayer: "Wake up in another book. On a kinder page" ('XIV').

City of Departures by Helen Tookey similarly presents itself as being written into a landscape, often European, sometimes Northern, and this landscape too is edited by memory and imagination. Spaces can not only change, but be erased:

> When we reached the sea-front I was at a loss. The front as I had known it – the busy road with its hotels and coloured lights, the children's boating lake with its blue and yellow paddle-boats – was no longer there.
>   ('Front')

Rational explanations are offset by hints of the unheimlich: "But it hasn't been like that for a very long time, they said. Not since *before*". Wrecks go missing, time pops itself out of joint, the scale of things seems wrong, as in one of several poems about the painter Leonora Carrington:

> You were the smallest, but now you've grown bigger
> so you pick them up between thumb and forefinger
>
> – mother, father, brother, brother –
> and fix them all in the painting, whistling
>   ('Leonora')

The book combines poems and prose poems in a compelling zone of stark atmospheres and richly observed interiors: hotels, seemingly empty; civic spaces where rhododendrons conspire with the signage; landscapes with artists fading into them. "As though the ordinary business of *being a hotel* were the discourse, which has suddenly been abandoned, the notional *hotel* turning instead to address us" ('Hotel Apostrophe').

These spaces become the set for found voices, the letters of Paul Celan and Ingeborg Bachmann in 'What Can We Still Do' echoing the voice of Vivienne Eliot in 'The Waste Land'. In the remarkable essayistic final section, 'Skizzen / Sketches', the roles of the artists and writers is considered not, as might be imagined, in terms of their cultural authority, but rather as genii locorum. Anita Rees for instance is described as merging with the island in North Frisia where she commits suicide: "She abstracted herself, eroded herself, erased herself, walked further and further into the island until she didn't come out."

Paradoxically, these erasures become types of transfiguration, ecstasies which affirm our at-homeness even as we depart. This is enacted in poem after poem – the girl "who chooses not to speak" ('Paper Birds') but to make origami birds, or the absent Louise imagined "pulling a sled across miles of snow, skirting the pinewoods" ('Louise'). Finally, in 'Quend-Plage-les-Pins', place is stripped of every human attribute, "the pines / can stay, and the dunes, with their strange / tenacious grasses", leaving only our ability to imagine it: "It wouldn't need / a name. It wouldn't need us."

W.N. Herbert's new collection The Wreck of the Fathership *will be published by Bloodaxe in 2020.*

SMALL VENUES

Joe Carrick-Varty, Somewhere Far, *Smith/Doorstop*, £5,
ISBN 9781912196692
Conor Cleary, priced out, *The Emma Press*, £6.50,
ISBN 9781912915255
Martha Kapos, Smile Variations, *HappenStance*, £5,
ISBN 9781910131572
Rebecca Perry, beaches, *Offord Road*, £6,
ISBN 9781999930462
Katherine Towers, The Violin Forest, *HappenStance*, £5,
ISBN 9781910131589

Meryl Pugh on the intimate space of the pamphlet

. . .

As these five publications demonstrate, the pamphlet is a flexible form. It can – amongst other functions – serve as a calling card for emerging writers; it can give a home to work that is separate from other, larger projects, or provide a first encampment for poems eventually housed in a book.

Firstly then, the pamphlet-as-calling-card, where the debut poet must balance pressure to demonstrate poetic skill against their own imperatives. Joe Carrick-Varty is a 2017/18 winner of Smith Doorstop's New Poets Prize. The poems in *Somewhere Far* are saturated with loss, often speaking directly to an absent father whose presence, paradoxically, is everywhere, haunting streets, pubs and betting shops, French doors or bodies of water, who possesses a pigeon and makes feathers fall from the sky. Other losses also pervade this slim volume; houses and flats are left behind as relationships falter and end; reality and memory – the everyday and imaginary – overlay and blur, evoking the disorientation of grief, as in 'When you lean close and tell me': "horses drinking from the lake of my father's face". Like the wheelbarrow "full to bursting with feathers I didn't ask for" ('Feathers'), these poems carry the vivid pain of loss and difficult relationships, even while enacting the necessary agony of letting go. Moving an abandoned bike, long colonised by the garden's small creatures, the speaker meets resistance as the grass "let[s] go with a small rip", like "a fist so intent on keeping hold" ('Your Bicycle'). That fist – hand as instrument of violence or safekeeping – embodies all that's at stake.

In Conor Cleary's *priced out*, a personable voice, evenly-paced lines and the frequent, hospitable use of regular stanzas invite the reader to wonder at all we take for granted in contemporary, Western life, be it pineapples, bees or the curios – historical or otherwise – thrown up by Vine and Twitter. A quiet humour is at work; two lovers "bumble / into one another" and "let out / a little whoop / like polite arthropods" ('collision'), while in 'The Mousse', the suitor-as-dessert admits they are "Not even my own / cup of tea". The accomplished title sequence explores the impact of economic volatility and the sense of being contingent on a life that is offered and visible but unattainable.

A careful tenderness beguiles in Cleary's poems, as in the eighth sonnet: "his dark eyes his hair his voice when exercised deliberately / are another shape of language altogether" ('Priced Out'). To want more seems churlish, but I did: perhaps a bit less orderliness, more "fistfuls of robins" and "outbursts" like those of the "old god" (who may also be human), cast to the margins and "impoverished by cities" in the rangy lines of 'wild divine'. Carrick-Varty and Cleary should be confident of their precise image- and verse-making; I'd encourage them towards less assiduous scene-setting, to trust in the reader's ability to infer, and more boldness in experimenting with form and syntax. I look forward to future work from both.

Martha Kapos is the author of three previous collections and until recently served as co-editor of *Poetry London* magazine. *Smile Variations* considers the ways in which our childhood experiences live inside us as adults, imbuing the material world with a potency that can appear at any moment. Even before invoking Proust ('madeleine'), this pamphlet clearly signals its concern with memory:

> I see   I saw   I see   I saw
> up to now   down to then   up to now
>>> ('See-saw with Woodpigeon and Crow')

There is meticulous attention to the things of the world that occupy the gaze. Objects threaten, actions alarm: a child in bed hears sounds "behind walls", aware of "the dark theatre of the living room // where her parents sit, he facing her across the coffee table // the loud surface crowded with household goods" ('Night Music').

This attention turns inward, too, upon cognition:

> Something is placing a chord
> on her tongue
>
> [...]
>
> It is fearfully soft. It reminds her
>
> – of the morning the arriving sun
> stopped in its tracks
>>> ('Between Major and Minor')

The exact placement of these short lines makes thought's occurrence tangible, as realisation opens into memory. Throughout, Kapos deploys stanza and line break to great effect. For example:

> How
> brave she
> is setting out
> endangered among the furniture
>>> ('To Her Father')

The incremental increase in line lengths and the enjambments' syntactical disruptions perform the child's fear and tenacious longing for "the rare / nod of approval". Later:

A spot of embattled

light
is seated
at the piano.

As with that earlier choice of "endangered", the use of "embattled" is apt and unusual and its dislocation from its object via both line and stanza break intensifies the sense of precariousness and effort. This formal precision extends to the pamphlet's arc: the first poem, with its exhortation to "fall / down if you down will fall" ('Into the Story') is echoed satisfyingly in the last: "The word might trip off her tongue / and fall out of the story" ('Fall Poem').

Rebecca Perry, whose first collection appeared in 2015, exploits the pamphlet's potential to control and intensify thematic unity. In the fourteen poems of *beaches*, a speaker stalks a coastline, seeking recovery from emotional damage and recalling a self from before, which like a cave "had another form / before the water came" ('beaches (3)'). The beaches offer distraction and small respite from the loneliness of houses "large and dark / with narrow rooms" ('beaches (2)') and the self's perceived failings. They are also a path towards agency and beyond. A man is pinned beneath a truck and the speaker, around whom "ladies whisper in corridors", has the head of "a yet to be identified / woodland creature / most likely a muntjac" ('beaches (9)'). That apparently casual "most likely" is unnerving when wedded to such transformations and injuries; this is characteristic of Perry's manipulation of tone into something excitingly discordant in its ironic detachment.

From agency to power: strangeness and danger erupt in 'beaches (10)', where hair grows independently of its owner and war and ghosts share space with "a cooked peacock [that] sits on the table folded back inside its feathers". The eruption is textual too, the pamphlet's habitually short lines mutating into longer ones that speed across the page, leaping the breaks created by white space.

This is welcome. Perry's short lines can be effective in conveying unease – "laughter / as the crabs boil" ('beaches (7)') – or may glint with haiku-like, concentrated focus:

a few paces on
brand new
early december roses

('beaches (6)')

But in the confined space of a pamphlet, any repeated poetic strategy promising coherence can equally risk monotony, so occasionally the effect is less successful:

I walked to the water
to wash
to relocate my voice

('beaches (4)')

Here, irony and sincerity struggle together as the emphatic landing of each short utterance tends towards bathos. Perhaps that's the intention, evoking as it might the heaviness of living in the mundane "real", while longing for "our liquid selves". Either way, my quibbles are outweighed by enjoyment: Perry's diction is original, the poems are studded with striking images and her eye is intelligently, sharply alert.

In Katherine Towers's third publication, a sympathetic, enquiring intelligence considers the natural world via strongly sensory images. Sparrows "bump and chink [...] like / small clay pots", comforting their observer: "I take to heart that busy fragrant dark, their kingliness and ease" ('Sparrows'). As those pots and kingliness suggest, this is a nature mediated by culture (the pamphlet abounds with references to music, dance and poetry) and by language. For Towers, this is inevitable: "We use the world to put our language / into use". Just so, this pamphlet puts the world to use for illumination and comfort:

Imagine a real garden where I sit
with my soul in dead November leaves,
thinking of your good words, like fox
and bower and bramble.

('The Good Words')

This response to W.S. Graham's 'Approaches to How They Behave' exemplifies these poems' clear-eyed, nuanced artfulness. They acknowledge the limits of language's reach and nature's independence from it – "Take from a river any thought of endlessness / or death to find it's only water on its way" – and remind us of our bond to the world in our own creatureliness. 'Green Thought', the pamphlet's final poem, confronts us with "that infecting fern", "blotched with spores you mustn't breathe", yet urges us to "[b]reathe in deep. There's nowhere else to live".

Meryl Pugh's first collection Natural Phenomena *(Penned in the Margins, 2018) was a PBS Spring Guest Selection.*

CONTRIBUTORS

Amy Acre has published two pamphlets, *And They Are Covered in Gold Light* (Bad Betty Press) and *Where We're Going, We Don't Need Roads* (flipped eye) • **Anne Barngrover** is the author of *Brazen Creature* (University of Akron Press, 2018); she lives in Tampa, Florida • **Liz Berry**'s books are *Black Country* (Chatto, 2014) and *The Republic of Motherhood* (2018) • **Paula Bohince** received second prize in the 2013 National Poetry Competition. Her most recent collection is *Swallows and Waves* (Sarabande, 2016) • **Natalie Linh Bolderston** won the silver Creative Future Writers' Award in 2018. Her pamphlet, *The Protection of Ghosts*, is published with V Press • **Piotr Florczyk**'s books include *East & West*, a collection of poems, and several volumes of translations • **Cheryl Follon**'s latest poetry collection is *Santiago* (Bloodaxe, 2017). She lives in Glasgow • **Alan Gillis** is a poet and critic based in Edinburgh and author of four collections from Gallery Press. A new collection will be published by Picador in 2020 • **Tom Hicks** is a Black Country photographer whose work can be seen at tomhicksphoto.com • **Jerzy Jarniewicz** is a Polish poet, translator and literary critic, who lectures at the University of Łódz. He has published twelve volumes of poetry and thirteen critical books on contemporary Irish, British and American literature • **Maria Johnston** is a poetry critic, lecturer and editor; she is co-editing a collection of essays on Irish women poets for 2020 publication • **Victoria Kennefick**'s pamphlet, *White Whale* (Southword, 2015), won the Saboteur Award for Best Poetry Pamphlet • **Anja Konig** grew up in the German language and now writes in English. Her first full collection will be published by Bad Betty Press in 2020 • **Nick Laird** is a writer-in-residence at New York University and Professor at the Seamus Heaney Centre, Belfast. *Feel Free* (Faber, 2018) was shortlisted for the T.S. Eliot Prize • **Thomas Lynch** is the author of five books of poems. His new essay collection *The Depositions* (W.W. Norton) is published in the US this winter • **Soumyaroop Majumdar** is a poet from Kolkata, India, currently studying for a PhD in Creative Writing at Durham University • **John McAuliffe**'s new collection *The Kabul Olympics* will be published by The Gallery Press in April 2020 • **Alice Miller**'s collection *Nowhere Nearer* (Pavilion, 2018) was a PBS Recommendation. She is a New Zealander based in Berlin • **Kim Moore**'s first collection *The Art of Falling* was published by Seren in 2015 and won the Geoffrey Faber Memorial Prize • **Penny Newell** holds a Northern Writers' Award and is a Visiting Lecturer in Creative Writing at Leeds Arts University. Her poems have appeared in various journals • **Jeremy Noel-Tod** teaches at the University of East Anglia and is the editor of *The Penguin Book of the Prose Poem* (2018) • **Richard O'Brien** is the Birmingham Poet Laureate 2018 2020. His pamphlets include *The Emmores* (The Emma Press, 2014) and *A Bloody Mess* (Valley Press, 2015) • **Meredi Ortega** is from Western Australia and now lives in Aberdeen. She won third prize in the Troubadour Prize 2018 • **Don Paterson** received the Queen's Gold Medal for Poetry in 2010. His new collection *Zonal* will appear from Faber in spring 2020 • **Padraig Regan** is the author of two pamphlets, *Delicious* (Lifeboat, 2016) and *Who Seemed Alive & Altogether Real* (The Emma Press, 2017). They live in Belfast • **Maurice Riordan**'s most recent collection of poems is *The Water Stealer* (Faber, 2013) • **Jaya Savige** was born in Sydney and lectures at the New College of the Humanities, London. He is the author of two collections and a third, *Change Machine*, will be published in 2020 • **Kathrin Schmidt** is a German poet and prose writer. Her latest collection *waschplatz der kühlen dinge* (2018) addresses globalisation and migration using the language of politics, advertising and the internet • **Phoebe Stuckes** is from West Somerset. Her first full-length collection *Platinum Blonde* will be published by Bloodaxe in 2020 • **Sue Vickerman** is developing a cross-genre manuscript combining poetry, translation, translation theory and fiction. She is an editor at Naked Eye Publishing • **Jay G. Ying** is a writer, translator and critic based in Edinburgh. His pamphlet, *Wedding Beasts*, is published by Bitter Melon.

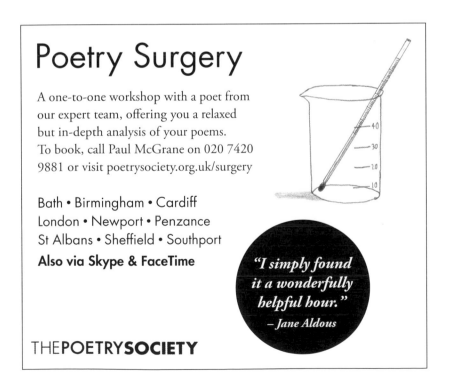

IP authenticated access to the world's best poetry quarterly
The Poetry Review digital

MULTI-USER ACCESS to an invaluable poetry archive

Get multi-user access for your organisation through an institutional subscription to the UK's leading poetry journal **The Poetry Review**.

Since it was founded in 1912, *The Poetry Review* has been home to the world's best writing – by both internationally renowned and emerging poets, newcomers and Nobel Prize winners. Subscriptions include the latest issue and a digital archive dating back to 2013. Access to the digital edition of *The Poetry Review* is optimised for library/institutional use:

- Delivered on the Exact Editions platform.
- IP authenticated access – no requirements to login with username and password.
- Remote/EzProxy access for registered users off site, as well as Shibboleth authentication.
- Fully searchable archive.
- Detailed statistical reporting provided in the administrator account.
- Extensive linking of each issue, inc. URLs, email addresses and page numbers.

For more information and to subscribe visit bit.ly/PoetryReviewdigital

SUBSCRIBE
TO *POETRY* TODAY

11 book-length issues

FREE VERSE

The Poetry Book & Magazine Fair 2020

Please join us at an all-day extravaganza of poetry publishing, readings and conversation. Browse a stall, buy a book, meet a friend, boost a publisher.

Sat 22 February 2020

Conway Hall
25 Red Lion Square
London WC1R 4RL
Nearest tube: Holborn

poetrybookfair.com

THE POETRY SOCIETY